WHEN THE BEGINNING ENDS
WHAT HAPPENS WHEN WE DIE?

PETER HECK

Copyright © 2017 by Peter Heck

All rights reserved. No part of this publication may be reproduced or transmitted in any form or by any means electronic or mechanical, including photocopy, recording, or any information storage and retrieval system now known or to be invented, without permission in writing from the publisher, except by a reviewer who wishes to quote brief passages in connection with a review written for inclusion in a magazine, newspaper, or broadcast.

Library of Congress Cataloging-in-Publication Data

ISBN-13: 978-1548707668
ISBN-10: 154870766X

Published in the United States by
Attaboy Press

a division of Attaboy Productions, Inc.
2139 Emily Court
Kokomo, IN 46902

For more information on Attaboy Productions, Inc., please visit:
www.peterheck.com

Distributed in cooperation with
CreateSpace
7290 B. Investment Drive
Charleston, SC 29418

To my brilliant brother Andrew and precious sister Katy. Your love for Christ is inspiring, and guarantees that growing up with me is the only Hell you will ever know.

CONTENTS

	Acknowledgments	i
1	Thinking About Death	1
2	You Will Die	7
3	Worms, Mumsi, & Limbo	14
4	What Death Means	21
5	Forget What You Feel	27
6	Grieve With Hope	38
7	The Shadow of Death	48
8	God Understands Reservations	55
9	Imagining the Unimaginable	62
10	What We Will See	68
11	What We Will Do	74
12	How We Will Feel	83
13	What About Our Spouse?	94
14	The King Has Come	101
15	Hell Matters	109
16	How We Feel About It	115
17	What God Says About It	122
18	Why Hell?	128
19	How You Get There	140
20	Glimpses of Hell	153
21	Social Torment	159
22	Physical Torment	167
23	Psychological Torment	175
24	How Could He?	184
	Citations	193

ACKNOWLEDGMENTS

As I mention in the opening chapter, I am so appreciative of the work and wisdom of so many great Bible scholars and teachers upon whom I relied in the compilation of this study. But special acknowledgement needs to go to Dr. Tony Evans of the Urban Alternative (TonyEvans.org) whose fascinatingly simple and straightforward teaching on "The Afterlife" was the impetus for this project and helped form the framework for this approach to understanding what the Bible says about the life to come.

ONE

THINKING ABOUT DEATH

"Is it starting to happen?"

That was the question a student of mine posed to me as he was walking out of my classroom at the end of the day. I had just finished explaining to his class why my customary teaching attire of khakis and a polo had been replaced with dark pants, shirt and tie. That day I was leaving from school to go to a funeral visitation of a friend who had died. It wasn't a close friend, but close enough that it was appropriate and proper to pay my respects.

"Is what starting to happen?" I asked back.

With a smirk he responded, "You're hitting that point in life where you are going to more funerals than weddings, aren't you?"

I threw my marker at him and told him if I wasn't

so apparently old and decrepit, I would run him down and pummel him for that remark.

But the truth is, he's not far off. If you go strictly by life expectancy rates, I'm not quite to the halfway point of my human existence. And despite what my punk student thinks, I am still more likely to check out movie showtimes in the newspaper than the obituaries when planning my social calendar. Yet thoughts of death are far more common for me now than they ever used to be.

Nearly every month I am hearing about someone I know personally who has died. Add to that the daily news reports of car accidents, homicides, or terrorist attacks, and the nagging thought of, "That could have been me." So if my student was intimating that death is on my mind a lot more these days, he couldn't have been more correct.

I don't want to be dead. I really like living.

But I'm going to be dead at some point, maybe sooner, maybe later. And it's no longer uncommon for me to make decisions based on the fact that we don't know how many tomorrows we get. Maybe it's the inevitability of death, or the unknown timing of it that intrigues me; maybe thinking about it is the way my subconscious copes with what I don't understand; or maybe it's something morbid in a mind that has seen way too many crime dramas and tear-jerker movies that draws me to the topic.

WHEN THE BEGINNING ENDS
WHAT HAPPENS WHEN WE DIE?

But I don't think it's any of that. I think that thinking about death is as natural as death itself. I think we are wired to think about death. And I think we're wired that way because the One who did the wiring *wants* us to think about death.

No, I'm not calling God dark or morose. He is everything the opposite of those things. He is life (John 14:6) – true life, vibrant life, pulsating life. And He knows what awaits us on the other side of these vaporous few years (James 4:14) is eternally more significant than the temporal things that consume far too much of our thinking here on this side of the grave.

We *should* be thinking about death and preparing for it far more than our weddings, what movies we're going to see, the careers we're going to have, or the retirement we want to enjoy. We *should* be obsessing about the preparations needed before death in comparison to the preparations needed before parties, picnics, and promotions.

Not because we are macabre. But because we wisely recognize what God has told us – the entirety of our existence on earth is merely the beginning of our life. Only a fool then would fail to think about what happens when the beginning ends.

I don't want to be a fool. I don't want you to be a fool. That is the motivation behind this project. But let me also be very clear what this work is and isn't.

(1) It is not the final authority on the issue of death, heaven, hell, and eternity.

Scholars and theologians far wiser, far more read and studied, far more articulate, and far more popular than I have written, taught, and lectured on these topics. And far more will continue to do so in the years to come. Listen to them, learn from them, and recognize that none of us have the mind of God. We are all capable of error in our understanding of these supernatural concepts.

(2) It is not my intent to weigh in on eschatology or debates surrounding end times prophecy. This book isn't about pre-millenialism, post-millenialism, the rapture, the thousand years, or even the book of Revelation.

(3) It is not a book about denominational doctrine. The research upon which I relied heavily to complete this work derives from a multitude of Christian denominational backgrounds, each with undoubtedly different takes on End Times issues.

For instance, I've drawn inspiration and instruction on the form, frame, and fundamental understandings I will write about in this book from an eclectic array of Christian thinkers like Dr. Tony Evans of the Urban Alternative (it was a message on the afterlife from Dr. Evans that first prompted me to begin this project, and his subsequent messages that

WHEN THE BEGINNING ENDS
WHAT HAPPENS WHEN WE DIE?

fueled the framework upon which I built my study), author Francis Chan, researcher Preston Sprinkle, theologian Jack Cottrell, and philosophers William Lane Craig and C.S. Lewis.

While those thinkers' backgrounds and beliefs would undoubtedly represent significant doctrinal distinctions, their research collectively points to a vividly clear understanding of the larger questions I address in this book. To be honest, it is both reassuring and encouraging to me that men of such varied denominational education and experience point with unanimity to many of the conclusions drawn in the following pages.

(4) This book is an attempt to articulate in a clear, relatable, and understandable way the answers to questions every human being will ask at some point in their existence:

- What happens when we die?
- Is there a heaven and what is it like?
- Is hell a literal place and is it eternal?

If you've never asked those questions or if they don't concern you, this book isn't for you. If you have and they do, I sincerely hope the following pages will prove a blessing and encouragement to your faith.

(5) What you are about to read is predicated entirely on the authority of the Bible. For reasons I will expound upon in the pages to

come, I view the Bible as the only authoritative and reliable voice on issues of a supernatural afterlife. I've sought to eliminate the conjecture and speculation, the guesses and assumptions of man, and offer a straightforward case for what the Bible says about what happens next.

If you do not trust the Bible to be the authoritative, infallible, inerrant Word of the One Creator God, this book will likely disappoint your craving for diverse views, opinions, and predictions.

The guesses of mortal men do not interest me. This is a book about answers.

TWO

YOU WILL DIE

I can only imagine that it started out as a completely routine day for Harry Ramos as he woke up, showered, shaved, ate his breakfast, dressed, and headed out the door for his stockbroker job on the 87th floor of the World Trade Center...on September 11, 2001. The actions of 19 Muslim terrorists in the next few hours would prevent him from ever coming home.

Victoria Soto undoubtedly had a similar predictable morning, albeit with likely a bit more excitement than Harry. After all, she was a young teacher getting the opportunity of a lifetime to lead her own classroom of sweet, innocent first graders, all eager to impress her. She rushed out the door and headed off to Sandy Hook Elementary School...on December 14, 2012. Less than two hours later, Victoria's final act would be trying to shield her little angels from a madman.

I can picture southerner Lynn Freeman walking to her car amazed at the late spring snowstorm that enveloped her while visiting Wyoming. She might have even thought about not traveling, but most likely reasoned that even if she wasn't used to it, this type of weather was nothing new there, and surely the roads would be passable. She drove slowly to the entrance ramp of I-80…on April 20, 2015. Moments later, two trucks would collide and jackknife across both westbound lanes, triggering a deadly chain reaction pile-up of dozens of cars, including Lynn's.

The ancient words of Scripture declare the inevitable truth of humanity: *It is appointed for men to die once* (Hebrews 9:27).

There's no escaping it, there's no denying it, there's no avoiding it. We can euphemistically characterize it however we want. And we do. Some of the soft terms and phrases humanity employs to escape stating the stark reality of death are extraordinary.

- He breathed his last
- He ceased to be
- He passed
- He passed away
- He crossed over
- He has departed
- He expired
- He is no more

WHEN THE BEGINNING ENDS
WHAT HAPPENS WHEN WE DIE?

- He has perished
- He is resting in peace
- He has succumbed
- He slipped away
- He went the way of all flesh

And then there the less soft phrases, that seek to assuage the reality of death with humor instead:

- He's at room temperature
- He bit the big one
- He bit the dust
- He cashed in his chips
- He checked into the Horizontal Hilton
- He's taking a dirt nap
- He kicked the oxygen habit
- He's been liquidated
- He's no longer counted in the census
- He took a permanent vacation

But no amount of humor or euphemistic phrasing can obscure this blunt truth: we are all headed for a destiny that ends in the grave. I used to work maintenance and grounds for a guy who spent two decades as a state cop. He always said the hardest part of his job was knocking on doors to inform a family about the death of a loved one. I was intrigued that police officers went through specific training on how to conduct an encounter like that – training that included strict instructions to use plain, simple, and candid language: "I regret to inform you that there's been an accident and your son is dead."

Not, "There's been an accident and your son was involved." Not, "I've just come from a wreck involving your daughter and she's not okay." Greg always said the words were to be honest and straightforward; that anything less than that was cruel.

I think there's a lesson there for us. It's cruel and inhumane to ignore the reality of death for not just ourselves, but for everyone around us. If Scripture is right that we all have an appointment with death, then despite our habits on earth, we can't delay, take a rain check, skip, or be late to this appointment. Trying to cope by believing that we can is tragically risky.

I recently read that one of the lead minds behind the online search giant Google is planning on beating death. Ray Kurzweil, hired in 2012 as a Director of Engineering at Google following his astonishingly successful career in pioneering computer technology, identifies himself as a "futurist." Widely regarded as one of the world's foremost thinkers and inventors, Kurzweil prides himself in his ability to accurately predict the future of technology and science. And in a 2016 interview with Playboy Magazine, Ray put forward his thoughts of the future of death:

> "By the 2030s we will have nanobots that can go into a brain non-invasively through the capillaries, connect to our neocortex and basically connect it to a synthetic neocortex that works the

WHEN THE BEGINNING ENDS
WHAT HAPPENS WHEN WE DIE?

same way in the cloud. So we'll have an additional neocortex, just like we developed an additional neocortex 2 million years ago, and we'll use it just as we used the frontal cortex: to add additional levels of abstraction. We'll create more profound forms of communication than we're familiar with today, more profound music and funnier jokes. We'll be funnier. We'll be sexier. We'll be more adept at expressing loving sentiments."[1]

Supposedly, this artificial life will allow human beings to eliminate death from our to-do list. And since Kurzweil thinks it will happen by the 2030s, he is doing all he can to sustain himself until then. And by "all he can," I mean eating a daily breakfast that includes berries, dark chocolate infused with espresso, smoked salmon and mackerel, vanilla soy milk with stevia, porridge, and Green tea. He's as rigidly committed to this morning meal as I am to my Little Debbie Fudge Round and Ocean Spray Cranapple.

Kurzweil doesn't offer any information on what he eats for other meals (or if he eats other meals at all). But he does supplement his diet with approximately 100 pills a day that costs him nearly $1 million a year.[2] That's a lot of Flintstones vitamins.

And yet, nanobots, neocortexes, and reanimation

talk aside, Ray Kurzweil is going to die. No amount of money changes that.

For as much as life is divided across social classes, death is not that way. It's the great equalizer. If you put the remains of a rich man's mausoleum next to the remains of a poor man's unmarked grave, you couldn't tell one set of bones from the other. Consider the beginning of the story of the rich man and the beggar Lazarus that Jesus tells His followers:

> *There was a rich man who was dressed in purple and fine linen and lived in luxury every day. At his gate was laid a beggar named Lazarus, covered with sores and longing to eat what fell from the rich man's table. Even the dogs came and licked his sores.*
>
> *The time came when the beggar died and the angels carried him to Abraham's side. The rich man also died and was buried. In Hades, where he was in torment, he looked up and saw Abraham far away, with Lazarus by his side* (Luke 16:19-23).

Notice that there is a difference between Lazarus and the rich man when they are living, and there is a difference between Lazarus and the rich man in the afterlife. But when it comes to death, they are as equal as it gets. Both die.

WHEN THE BEGINNING ENDS
WHAT HAPPENS WHEN WE DIE?

And perhaps there's one other point that bears emphasis before we lay this uncomfortably frank chapter to rest. Death will eventually render us irrelevant here on earth. I don't remember who the first preacher or speaker was that I heard offer this challenge, but sometimes I will use it when addressing congregations or conventions: name your great, great grandma.

Not by the nickname she was given by her grandkids, but by her real name. Can you do that on the spot with no research? Can you honestly say that you spend much time thinking about your great, great grandma as you go throughout your daily routine? Can you honestly say that until this moment you have ever thought about her once in your entire life?

There's no shame in that – it's a simple truth about death we shouldn't overlook. Regardless of how important you may think you are now, the grave has a way of turning us all into irrelevance. Once you've been gone for a period of time, there's not a soul on earth who will ever remember you were here.

In light of that fact, just set the $100 vitamins to the side for a minute and keep reading.

THREE

WORMS, MUMSI, & LIMBO

I'm glad you turned the page. Because with as uncomfortable as it may make us to acknowledge that we all have an imminent and unavoidable rendezvous with death, the question it provokes is profound: "then what?"

If you listen around you, plenty of folks are ready to tell you what they think. Take astrophysicist Neil DeGrasse Tyson, a man who enjoys talking so much that even if he doesn't know an answer, he will delight you with a 20-minute soliloquy explaining why you were an idiot for asking him in the first place. Famed television anchor Larry King (who himself has had plenty of brushes with death in his 284 years on earth) asked Tyson, "What do you think happens when we die?" Tyson responded:

"Put me in the ground. Let the worms,

WHEN THE BEGINNING ENDS
WHAT HAPPENS WHEN WE DIE?

microbes, come in and out of my body, and the energy content of my body, that I had assembled, over my lifetime consuming the flora and fauna of this earth. My body then returns to them and thus is the cycle of life. I *know* that's gonna happen because you can measure where the energy goes. And that's how I wanna go out."

Of course, that didn't answer King's question at all. Nor did it shed any new light on what we already knew happened during decomposition of the physical body. This is what Tyson does better than anyone else – use so many words to say nothing at all. Frustrated, King tried a more direct approach, asking, "You're not conscious, and that's for eternity, right?"

Acting almost insulted by the silliness of the question, Tyson stammered, "Uh yeah, there's no evidence that I have any consciousness of anything."[1] Thanks, Neil.

Dr. Brian Weiss offered a different perspective on what happens after death, saying, "I think that we never die because we're never really born."

Say what?

The psychiatrist and hypnotist went on:

"We existed before. You existed before this birth. You were probably a spirit guide to your mother or someone else. You were on the other side. Then you come into a physical body as a baby, and you go through life, and the next stage though is leaving the body. So if you are the soul, you never die. When the body dies, you go on."[2]

While giving his take, atheist author and speaker Hemant Mehta picked up on that same parallel to existence prior to birth, only in the gloomy, hopeless, futile sense you would expect from those who believe there's no meaning behind life:

"Well, where were you before you were born? You weren't around. It's not like you were in pain. It's not like you were in elation. You were just not there. And that's what's gonna happen when you die. You're just no longer there.

And that's not a good thing or a bad thing, it's just a part of life, really. And I think what we can hope for is that you've left behind a legacy of some sort. That your physical body is not gonna be there anymore, but hopefully your memories will be and people will still talk about you, and remember you. And that's probably the best we can all hope for."[3]

WHEN THE BEGINNING ENDS
WHAT HAPPENS WHEN WE DIE?

Well what a ray of sunshine that is, Hemant. Do you suppose Hemant has ever been asked if he can name his great, great grandma?

If Mehta's atheist despair is a little too despondent for you, there's always the upbeat prediction of inspirational speaker and New Thought life coach Ilyana Vanzant who had this exchange with The Oprah:

> The Oprah: What happens when we die?
>
> Ilyana: We just keep going, it just looks different. We just, it's here! I, you know, I can't think what happens when we die, I have to imagine what happens when we die. And I think it's like we just wake up the next day in someplace and continue on what we (sic) doing.
>
> The Oprah: Mmmm.
>
> Ilyana: I don't think it's the end and the darkness and all that. And for me, again, back to my Master Teacher Jameya. About a week after she died and I was in

>
> the shower weeping my heart out. And I said, "Oh Jameya where are you?" And she said, "I'm right here Mumsi."

The Oprah: That's what I believe. I believe they're all right here.

Ilyana: Mmhmm.[4]

With all due respect to Mumsi, perhaps something a little less reliant on grief-filled shower encounters and more grounded in science would be helpful? And even though he's not a real scientist, Bill Nye played one on TV. Here were his enlightening thoughts on the issue:

> "Now when it comes to life after death, I've thought about this quite a bit. What happens? What are you like when you're dead? If you watch people age like my grandmother, my beloved grandmother …I just don't see any evidence that she would suddenly be a young person as an after-dead ghost entity. It looks like, to me, this life is all you get. This is it. There's nothing afterwards."[5]

Finally, what about more of an artistic mind, like lyricist Paulo Coelho, who shares a vivid expectation of heaven and a god who asks but one question upon our entrance there:

> "And God in my opinion, is going to ask only one question. God's not asking, uh 'Did you sin a lot, did you do this, did you do that?' God is going to ask you only one question, that it is (sic), 'Did you love enough?' And if you say yes, welcome to heaven. If you say no, you are in the limbo."[6]

Now I like a good game of limbo as much as the next guy, but I'm thinking that admissions process might be a bit flawed. It seems like the answer to give God is, "You bet, absolutely, I was a lover, God!" And I wonder if Paul thinks we can update our answer after we get tired of "the limbo" or if we're locked in that game for eternity? He didn't specify unfortunately.

So you get the picture:

- The atheist tells us confidently that there's nothing on the other side.
- The universalist tells us hopefully that there is a heaven waiting on the other side and we are all going. After all, a loving God couldn't send anyone to Hell – it would be contrary to His nature!
- The Eastern meditation guru and new age philosopher preach reincarnation and the state of perpetual existence.
- The pagan offers that some vague, spiritual ghost of you moves into the underworld.

All of these various theories are incredibly diverse, and yet they all have one crucial detail in common with one another: they are all remarkably uninformed opinions. Oh I know that men like Tyson have more degrees than men like Coelho. And it's true that someone like Dr. Weiss has more wisdom and experience in his little finger than someone like Mehta. But not a single one of these sources is speaking from a position of authority.

Not one of them can offer the testimony of a mind that has been to the other side of the grave and come back. So for those who think I'm being unfairly dismissive of their theories, I admit I'm guilty. They're just not good enough for me.

Now, if these kinds of guesses interest you, more power to you. If you're intrigued by creative speculations, these are just some of hundreds you can choose from – or you can make up your own.

But as I've already told you, I'm not interested in guesses. I'm interested in answers. And I'm not interested in wasting your time with my uninformed opinions either. With what is riding on this question, I really can't afford for the person I believe to be wrong. And if you're reading this book, you may be inclined to believe me. Which means you can't afford for me to be wrong.

FOUR

WHAT DEATH MEANS

It's because of my demand for truth and not conjecture that I won't accept the predictions about the afterlife from someone who has never experienced the afterlife. That should make sense to all of us. We don't believe someone who says:

- something tastes good unless they've eaten it before.
- a movie isn't scary unless they've watched it before.
- how a medication will make us feel unless they've taken it before.

And that's where I am on the afterlife. I am not going to believe someone who tells me what it's going to be like if they've never been there before. That's why you see so many people gravitate towards books like *Heaven is for Real* or *23 Minutes in Hell*. We are looking for an authoritative voice of someone who has experienced what they claim to know.

It's also why I am overly selective, perhaps annoyingly so, about who and what I will read regarding the topic. If the author or speaker doesn't pass this simple test of humility, I won't give anything they say much credibility. If they don't admit this, I don't want to listen:

I don't know what is going to happen when we die.

I need to hear that from you if you want me to regard what you have to say on the topic with any integrity.

Because no one we will encounter knows either. And the reason is simple: we've never died. We've never been in the grave, and we don't get to talk to anyone who has been.

Yes, people have had near-death experiences, they have "coded," they have been on the verge of physical expiration only to be brought back by medical expertise or the miraculous. But if someone is telling you what being dead was like, it means they weren't dead.

What I'm getting at is that any belief about the afterlife is predicated around faith. *Any* belief. Hemant Mehta and Bill Nye may be right that there isn't anything that happens — we just cease to exist. But they don't *know* that. And if they tell you they know that, they are liars. They have faith that is what

WHEN THE BEGINNING ENDS
WHAT HAPPENS WHEN WE DIE?

happens. Ilyana Vanzant and The Oprah may be right that dead bodies are invisible and all around us. But they don't *know* that. They have faith that is what happens.

And what I'm going to tell you in this book is something that I don't know for a fact either. I believe it is what happens because I have faith. And my faith is entirely predicated on my belief that the Bible bears the testimony of the only One who has been to the other side of the grave and come back to tell us about it. I believe that the Bible alone offers the authoritative voice on the topic that I so desperately need to hear from.

For a host of reasons I outline elsewhere and won't argue in this book, I believe that the Holy Bible, as compiled by the early church fathers, embodies the Divine revelation of the Creator of all to His created beings. I believe it is the authoritative Word of God Himself. I believe it offers the testimony of the Author of Life and Conqueror of Death. Therefore, what answers I offer in this book are merely a reflection of my understanding of what He told us.

I speak on His authority, not on the basis of my own thoughts. I'm stressing all this to the point of obnoxiousness because I want you to have your eyes opened about what you are reading since the stakes in this discussion are so high. As I said last chapter, if I dare to write on a topic like this, I need to do it with the humility to recognize you can't afford for me to be wrong. So I will let His word speak, and *let God be true and every man a liar* (Romans 3:4).

Back in Genesis 2, I think we can begin to understand what happens when we die a physical death here on earth. And it starts with how we were made by the Creator. The Creation account tells us, *Then the Lord God formed a man from the dust of the ground, and breathed into his nostrils the breath of life, and the man became a living being* (Genesis 2:7).

When you read that, a few things should jump out at you. First, God formed Adam's physical body, but he didn't become "alive" until God breathed into what He had formed. Adam was a physical entity, but he wasn't animated until the Creator animated it with His life-giving breath. In other words, Adam didn't become Adam until God gave him his soul.

The small town where I grew up and now teach has long had a joke about the shocking number of twins that go through our school system. There haven't been as many in recent years, but for awhile, there were sometimes up to ten sets of twins in our relatively small high school all at once. Jokes about what was in the water in Greentown were common.

One of the things that will stand out at you if you ever are around twins is how different they really are from one another. Even twins that get along and have that freakish "twin sense" that let's them anticipate the thoughts or actions of the other one in an uncanny way are so different in personality. It's honestly the easiest way for me to tell twins apart when I have them in class. I don't look for distinguishing physical characteristics like a mole or scar. I just get them talking and can quickly distinguish one from another.

This is the reality of the individual soul. Even human beings that share stunningly similar looks, shapes, body frames, and physical markings possess a distinct, and remarkably, miraculously unique soul.

Now, obviously God gives us both a spirit and a physical body for a reason. We are not to identify one as godly and the other as insignificant as some various Christian sects and pagan cultures have taught. Your physical body has purpose and is to be of use to God on earth. But it's helpful to our understanding of what happens at death to recognize that the physical body is the mortal container for the immortal soul that we received from God at the moment of conception (Psalm 51:5).

With that reality in mind, go back again and look at what Jesus tells us in that account of Lazarus the beggar: *The time came when the beggar died and the angels carried him to Abraham's side* (Luke 16:22). Do yourself a favor and look at the word that immediately follows "died" in this quote from Jesus. *And.* According to Scripture, there's something after death. According to the words of Jesus Himself, death is a conjunction, not a period.

When your eyes shut in physical death (provided you don't do that really freaky thing and die with your eyes open), it's not over. In fact, according to Jesus, you've only just begun. One of the things about the Word of God, whenever it talks about the physical death of humanity, it's critical to know what "dying" translates to in our language.

Dying doesn't mean "ceasing." It doesn't mean "ending." It doesn't mean "stopping." It doesn't mean "terminating." The word Jesus and His Scriptures use repeatedly for our "death" quite literally means "separation" (James 2:26). Perhaps Ecclesiastes offers the best description of this: *Then the dust will return to the earth as it was, and the spirit will return to God who gave it* (Ecclesiastes 12:7).

At the moment of death, then, our soul – quite literally the life that God breathed into us to animate our earthly flesh – separates from its mortal container (that's an admittedly utilitarian and unhelpful description of our physical body) and lives on.

According to the Author of Life, what happens when we die? Your body sleeps, your soul does not.

Now, thanks to Neil DeGrasse Tyson's vivid description of microbes and worms that we were blessed with in the last chapter, we know what becomes of the body. But the soul that has been separated from it has an entirely different destination.

FIVE

FORGET WHAT YOU FEEL

It comes as no surprise to anyone even remotely familiar with Scripture to learn that according to Jesus, upon the physical death of your body, your departed soul will be heading to one of two destinations. He made it perfectly clear to those gathered on the hillside to hear His famous Sermon on the Mount:

> *Enter through the narrow gate. For wide is the gate and broad is the road that leads to destruction, and many enter through it. But small is the gate and narrow the road that leads to life, and only a few find it.* (Matthew 7:13-14)

Two options: the small gate or the wide gate; the narrow road or the broad road; life or destruction. And He reiterated that truth throughout His ministry.

When giving us a glimpse of the afterlife, Jesus recounted this about the separated souls of Lazarus the Beggar and the rich man:

> *The time came when the beggar died and the angels carried him to Abraham's side. The rich man also died and was buried. In Hades, where he was in torment, he looked up and saw Abraham far away, with Lazarus by his side.* (Luke 16:22-23)

Two options: Abraham's side (sometimes translated "Abraham's bosom," or "with Abraham," but unquestionably referring to a state of paradise and eternal rest) or Hades (Hell). And notice in this story that the separated soul departed immediately for one of those two destinations. If we trust the Bible, we know that our souls will go one way or the other without delay.

Now, if you don't trust the Bible, you can create whatever vision of soul destination you want to – and many men have done that through the ages. There's the ancient Tibetan belief of a state called "Bardo."

Eastern religions teach the idea of reincarnation, where your soul is eternal and continues coming back from the dead, just housed in a different body, animal or entity. When you die in this life, your soul will be rehoused in a new body that is then born into the world. Bardo is where you go when you're dead, but you're waiting on that new body to be ready for business. It is full of spiritual subconscious phenomena as you anticipate your rebirth. I suppose some really enlightened guys came up with that idea.

Perhaps a little more familiar to Americans, and even American Christians, would be the concept of "soul sleep." This gets into End Times prophecy and eschatological timing – do souls reside in heaven now, or do they wait until Jesus comes back and resurrects every believer?

The philosophy of soul sleep teaches that upon physical death your soul exists only in the memory of God until He initiates the resurrection of the dead. At that point He puts your soul into its resurrected body for the rest of eternity. You allegedly have no consciousness or awareness of your condition during this duration of soul sleep. In other words, the souls of Jesus' disciples, as well as the soul of my Granny and every other departed believer are sound asleep right now, and they will have no idea they've been sleeping when the final trumpet sounds to wake them up. It's got a fascinating Sci-Fi feel to it. But it's not taught anywhere in the Bible. In fact, what Jesus teaches directly contradicts this idea.

As does the teaching of the most familiar "in-between" stage we hear about these days – purgatory. Purgatory is a popular teaching in the Catholic Church that suggests a staging area for human souls. It is a place populated only by Christians, but not all Christians must go there. Think of it this way: have you ever noticed that some Christians live worldlier lives than others? They've come to Christ and are believers, but they use profanity regularly, watch movies they shouldn't, don't always treat people the way they should?

This is likely a believer bound for Purgatory. Pure believers are admitted into heaven; but worldlier believers must make a pit-stop in Purgatory to become more purified. Everyone in Purgatory is bound for heaven, meaning none remain in that place of purification forever, and none who are there will ever be sent to Hell. But God needs to refine them a bit before they are ready to be brought into paradise. Again, it's an interesting theory and has been taught for centuries by men far smarter than me. But it's not in the Bible and it is not supported by what the Bible teaches.

I've made it clear that in this book I will only tell you what the Bible says. If you are convinced that God intentionally chose to leave out any reference to Purgatory, but instead enlightened future church leaders to introduce it as essential Christian doctrine, that's entirely your choice. As for me, I will speak only on the authority of the Scriptures compiled by the early church fathers, not on the authority of any later man or group of men.

And the authority of the words of Jesus tells us quite lucidly that upon death the soul is separated immediately and is delivered one of two places.

Now don't get me wrong. I understand why we may *want* to come up with alternative ideas or theories. I get why so many spiritual gurus of modern times make out like bandits when they begin proffering a theory of a universalist heaven where everyone makes it on their own terms, taking their own path. As self-serving, self-interested men (Isaiah 53:6) that's what we want to hear.

It's why the internet is populated with self-satisfying explanations of our eternal destiny that directly contradict the truth of Scripture, like this one offered by spiritualist Crystal Kernan:

> "There were many years I spent completely believing in Hell, being afraid of Hell. Being afraid if I did something wrong, if I transgressed bad enough, God my Father, God my Creator — no matter how much I loved Him — would send me to that place of eternal damnation and torment.
>
> Thank God I progressed beyond that somewhat infantile version or idea of who God is. Because that's not who God is. The whole notion of Hell is incongruent to the nature of God. The nature of God is love. God is goodness, God is righteousness. God is peace, God is harmony, God is balance. God is all good things. It is not logical to me that

a God who is all those good things, and a parent to us as Creator, would send us, His children, into a place of eternal torment and torture."[1]

I get it. I understand Crystal's desire to not feel like believing in God. But as my favorite Jewish commentator Ben Shapiro likes to say, "Facts don't care about your feelings." You are more than welcome to create a god that you want to worship. If that seems like a good idea to you, then by all means do so. But don't mistake your humanist ritual for Christianity. Paul is explicitly clear that God *is not served by human hands, as if he needed anything. Rather, he himself gives everyone life and breath and everything else* (Acts 17:25).

You and I know of God what He has chosen to reveal to us. When we go beyond that to try to reshape Him or reform Him to fit our own understandings and preferences, we have departed the counsel of Scripture (Proverbs 3:5-6) and are no longer practicing Christianity.

Forget what you feel. Trust what you're told.

We will get to what God tells us about Hell soon enough, but for now, look again where Jesus said Lazarus the Beggar was sent immediately:

> *The time came when the beggar died and the angels carried him away to Abraham's side* (Luke 16:22).

As I mentioned earlier, the best translation calls the place Lazarus went as "Abraham's bosom." This reference is only used in the New Testament, and is synonymous to when John rested his own head on Christ (John 13:23) while reclining around the table. Understood contextually, the phrase intimates rest – and in this case, is a clear reference to the eternal rest offered in paradise.

Leave it to human beings to take that glorious promise of eternal rest and conclude that heaven must be "boring." We imagine floating on a lonely cloud with our wings and halo looking around and wishing we had a cell phone to mess on or a book to read. One famous cartoonist depicted two angelic humans floating along looking forlorn and bored, while one looks at the other and says, "I miss stress."

Preachers don't even help with this misconception too much themselves. Almost every sermon I've heard on heaven talks about massive amounts of people all huddled around the throne of God singing "Holy, Holy, Holy" throughout eternity. I remember in college hearing a professor give that same description of heaven during a chapel service with the whole student body. I thought then what I think now: if you're trying to sell people on the magnificence of heaven, being crammed shoulder to shoulder in a sea of humanity, all singing the same thing over and over while standing before a King's throne, for a bazillion years isn't the way to do it.

Whenever I point that out to a minister they usually get defensive and say things like, "Well that's the great difficulty of trying to describe the indescribable." Not to be argumentative, because I do believe as mortal humans we are completely impotent to even attempt to put words to what is awaiting us in heaven. But if what you're describing to people sounds boring to them, then you should either find a better way of describing it or you should just stop trying.

Because what the Bible reveals about heaven tells us that there won't be a millisecond of boredom there. It tells us we won't have:

- An instant of frustration. No more being the one car in your lane that doesn't make it through the stoplight before it turns. No more switching grocery store aisles to get behind someone with fewer items only to have the register go down.
- A single sickness. No more nausea. No more headaches. No more allergies. No more pain.
- A hint of depression. No more feeling isolated when you are surrounded by people. No more confusion as to why you feel in a funk when you have every reason to be happy.
- A moment of aggravation. No more people eating with their mouths open. No more political posturing by celebrities or sports stars. No more couples sitting on the same side of the booth when there's a perfectly usable other side sitting empty.

WHEN THE BEGINNING ENDS
WHAT HAPPENS WHEN WE DIE?

The truth is that Scripturally, "eternal rest" would be better translated and understood "eternal enjoyment." We know that there is no night in heaven (Revelation 22:5), and that we are given new spiritual bodies for the experience (1 Corinthians 15:35-38). Have you paused to consider why that is? The answer is self-evident: so you never stop seeing it and never tire of experiencing it. Remember that's what we're promised in the age to come:

> *In order that in the coming ages He might show the incomparable riches of His grace* (Ephesians 2:7)

What does "incomparable" mean? Try to think of the best experience you've ever had. It's tough to do on the spot. It's tough to do when you're writing a book and have time to sit and think it through. But let me offer this as my example:

Not long ago, we went as a family to Walt Disney World in Florida. At the time, my children were 7, 5, and 3. My wife's parents came down to join us for a few days and offered to keep the kids one night back at our hotel room so Jenny and I could go enjoy ourselves. The kids were content and happy. The weather was perfect – mid 70s, gentle breeze, and dusk. Jenny and I went to the Magic Kingdom where there was virtually no crowd. We walked on ride after ride. We had a huge meal at our favorite place in the park. Later I had an ice cream sandwich that was bigger than my face, and she had a fruity-chocolate-waffle thingy that was twice the size of my ice cream sandwich. The lighting around the park was amazing, the sights and sounds were happy, and so were we. I will never forget that evening.

Thinking back on it even now, I can remember only two problems with the night: it was way too short, and my body got way too tired. I blame the earth's rotation for the first, and I blame the way my kids have aged me for the second. I'm guessing no matter what experience you came up with as your best ever, your problems might be the exact same two – you eventually wore out (or would have) and it eventually ended.

Now here's the truth about heaven: your best day here is Hell compared to your first moment in heaven. The experience of heaven will dwarf anything you've ever known. And the best part? It will never end, and you will never tire. It is truly incomparable, inexpressible, and inexplicable.

Sometimes when I peruse social media sites like Instagram or Snapchat, I will see fellow believers I follow on those apps post spectacular pictures of nature. Whenever there's a notably beautiful sunset in the area, you're guaranteed to see about 50 pictures of it appear that night on people's posts. They usually add a funny caption like "God Art" or "I see you doing work, God." But the truth is we have no idea. Paul writes as much to the Corinthians:

WHEN THE BEGINNING ENDS
WHAT HAPPENS WHEN WE DIE?

What no eye has seen, what no ear has heard, and what no mind has conceived, the things God has prepared for those who love Him (1 Corinthians 2:9).

Think about that. No eye has seen anything like what God is preparing for us. Take the most amazing sunset over a beach, the most breathtaking canyon with trees lining its valley, the most awe-inspiring mountain ranges, and it's not even approaching the realm of what heaven is like. We can't even conceive of it in our minds.

Which makes sense when you consider that His word tells us all those remarkable things we see and hear on earth, He put together in 6 days (Genesis 1). He's been working on preparing the next life for thousands of years. In light of that, I'm going to go ahead and hazard a confident guess that "boring" isn't a term we will likely ascribe to it.

Something inexplicable is awaiting us, and according to the Bible, it will be our reality before the coroner even pronounces us dead. Maybe that's why Scripture repeatedly avoids the use of the term "death" to describe the physical end for believers, opting instead for the word "asleep." As Dr. Tony Evans puts it, "Before your body even shuts its eyes, you are immediately transformed into the presence of God."[2]

I can't even imagine.

SIX

GRIEVE WITH HOPE

If all this is true — if we are truly ushered into unimaginable, inconceivable glory before our eyes even shut for the last time on earth, it can't help but alter how we Christians deal with death.

Scripture even tells us that we should *prefer to be away from the body and at home with the Lord* (2 Corinthians 5:8). But unless my experience is far different than every other Christian, I don't think those are words we really buy into or embrace. At least not until we are old, decrepit, and wasting away on our deathbed.

Not long ago my wife and I attended the funeral visitation for a wonderful woman from our church. Her death wasn't a surprise, but given that she was only in her mid 70s, it was still an understandably solemn occasion. As we made our way through the

WHEN THE BEGINNING ENDS
WHAT HAPPENS WHEN WE DIE?

long line and approached the casket, all of a sudden over the dull murmur of the 100 or so people sitting and waiting patiently to pay their respects, I heard my minister's voice booming out something unintelligible, followed by a his hearty laugh.

Jenny and I both turned around and looked, as did a few other folks – all of us undoubtedly thinking the same thing: "Geez Dave, dial it down a notch, you're at a funeral for heaven's sake." After we hugged the family and turned to leave, I ran into Dave (who was still loudly and joyously working the crowd) and I sarcastically smirked, "Hey, Jocko, I'm not sure if you were aware, but we've got a funeral going on in here." He wrapped his gigantic right arm around me and answered, "What are you talking about, brother?! This is a celebration!"

I nodded and smiled, we talked for a bit, and then Jenny and I left. The truth is that he gave a very minister-ish answer. That's what he's supposed to say, after all. But it's pretty evident from most of the Christian funerals I've attended, many of us who should believe what he's saying is true, really struggle to live like it is.

Funerals are sad events, marked by sad songs, sad readings, sad recollections, and sad people saying their goodbyes to someone they don't want to say goodbye to. We put the person we love dearly in one of their favorite outfits, lay them in a box, pay someone to try to make their face look full of life when it is no longer there, and parade everyone they knew by the box in a way that prompts tears and a sense of closure. If no one else will say it, I will. It's weird. It's a weird thing we do. I don't know who started it or when and why they did – but it's weird.

And even though I'm not going to push for some kind of anti-funeral movement within the church, and even though I will participate in this bizarre tradition myself, I do think it's worth pointing out that our funeral services may actually do a disservice to believers and unbelievers alike. For Christians, if we aren't careful, the funeral service can facilitate a kind of grieving that Christ-followers are to have no part in. And for non-Christians, our opportunity to witness to them by setting ourselves apart from the hopelessness they feel marching into Christ-less graves is squandered when we emote the same despairing sentiments.

I think that's precisely why Paul – the greatest evangelist of all time – placed so much emphasis on this point when he wrote, *We do not want you to be uninformed about those who sleep in death, so that you do not grieve like the rest of mankind, who have no hope* (1 Thessalonians 4:13). If there is not a palpable, noticeable difference between worldly funerals and Christian funerals, then we would be wise to get out of the funeral business altogether.

Being a teacher, I have had plenty of students from a wide variety of beliefs and backgrounds. And through the years, many of them have lost family members and I have gone to the visitation or funeral to show my respect and love for the young kid whose life has been abruptly altered by the loss. That's put me at a lot of funerals of non-Christians. And to date, they are almost all exactly the same; every single one has been focused exclusively on the past.

The families will share their memories; they will raise a toast to the good times they had with the dear departed; they will talk about how from now on when they drink this, eat that, chew this, or smoke that, they'll always be thinking about the dead person. The hired minister will then say a prayer, or maybe make a false promise of how they'll all meet again, and that's it. The tears don't stop until enough alcohol has been imbibed to dull the senses, or somebody starts to entertain to take the group's mind off death.

This is how the world grieves – as those who have no hope. Far too many Christian funerals border on that same mood. Far too many focus only on what has been lost, or what has been left behind. Far too many only give lip service to what "one day" will be. Far too few actually address what is happening *that very moment* in paradise. Once I would love to go to a funeral where the message was all about Heaven and what my loved one was doing at that very second.

If you think that I'm making too big of a deal out of this, or that I shouldn't let it bother me so much, let's remember that it bothered Jesus too. I think the two most famous Bible verses come from the same book of John. Thanks to the signs held up by fans in the end zone during extra points and field goals of every professional football game, most of the world is familiar with John 3:16. But running a close second has to be the shortest verse in the Bible, *Jesus wept* (John 11:35).

Everyone knows it as the shortest verse, but very few actually know all the reasons why Jesus wept. The account where it occurs involves the death of Christ's good friend Lazarus. It was the home of Lazarus and his sisters Mary and Martha that Jesus would often stop and visit when He was in town. When Jesus gets word that Lazarus is sick, He doesn't drop everything and rush to the scene. In fact, he delays a bit before going; long enough of a delay that Lazarus dies. When Jesus finally decides to head towards Bethany, the hometown of His friends, He tells His disciples,

> *"Our friend Lazarus has fallen asleep; but I am going there to wake him up." His disciples replied, "Lord, if he sleeps, he will get better." Jesus had been speaking of his death, but his disciples thought he meant natural sleep. So then he told them plainly, "Lazarus is dead, and for your sake I am glad I was not there, so that you may believe. But let us go to him."* (John 11:11-15)

WHEN THE BEGINNING ENDS
WHAT HAPPENS WHEN WE DIE?

Notice that Jesus called the condition of Lazarus *sleep* when He first explained His death. It wasn't until after His disciples were clearly confused that Jesus had to use the word death. What that tells me is that according to Jesus, *sleep* is the more accurate term for what has occurred, not *death*. If that is confusing, just recognize what happens when you are asleep. Your body is in an unconscious state; you aren't talking, walking, communicating, or moving, but you are still fully infused with life. The same is true after (what we call) physical death occurs. Your body is in an unconscious state, unable to talk, walk, communicate, or move, but you are still fully infused with life – either in heaven or hell.

The second thing to notice about what Jesus says is that He is *glad* He wasn't there when Lazarus fell into this sleep. Why in the world would He say such a heartless thing? Because it isn't heartless – Jesus is about to teach His disciples and us a valuable lesson in what it means to actually *believe* in Him.

I think most everyone of us can sympathize with Martha who meets Jesus when He finally strolls up to the scene. To put it plainly, she chews Him out:

- Where were you?!
- Why weren't you here?!
- You know, if you would have just come a little sooner this wouldn't have happened, right?!
- I thought you cared about us?!
- Yes, I know my brother will rise again in the last days when you come back, but he didn't need

to die now if you would have just showed up when we called for you!

Martha is just peppering Jesus with thinly veiled accusations and you can almost picture Christ calmly reaching up, grabbing her flailing hands, talking in hushed, calming tones as He says to her,

> *"I am the resurrection and the life. The one who believes in me will live, even though they die; and whoever lives by believing in me will never die. Do you believe this?"* (John 11:25-26)

Now, Scripture doesn't say this happened, so I can't prove it. But I can almost see Martha looking through her tears into the eyes of Jesus, Jesus pushing the tears away and saying again, "Do you believe?" Remember, that's exactly why He told the disciples He was glad Lazarus had died before He got there – so that they and everyone else there would *believe* in Him. Martha settled down and acknowledged the truth that her brother wasn't really dead – that he had merely been changed and transformed to live on, right at that very second.

Mary had a different reaction than Martha's rage and frustration. Mary was a mess. She fell at the feet of Jesus and cried out her pitiful plea, "Why?" It's not unlike the plea many of us make when we lose someone we love dearly:

- "Why him?"

- "Why now?"
- "Why of all people?"
- "Why did she have to leave us?"

Seeing her grief, the Bible says that the Jews who had come with her out to meet Jesus were also mourning and weeping. And it was at that moment, in that context, surrounded by all that sorrow from people who followed Him that we see Jesus weep.

But why? The Jews gathered there at that 1st century equivalent of a funeral for Lazarus thought they knew. When they saw Jesus crying, *the Jews said, "See how he loved him!"* (John 11:36). There's little doubt that being fully human, with fully human emotions, Jesus hated the pain being felt by His friends. As the all-knowing, all-feeling God, He could sympathize. As a mortal man, He could empathize.

For being the shortest verse in the Bible, there is a tremendous amount of depth in these two words. Because not only is Jesus experiencing the very real grief we humans encounter at the loss of a beloved family member or friend, but I believe His tears are infused with a righteous anger at the corruptive sin that makes this terrible process of death a necessity. It was never supposed to be that way, and Jesus (of all people) knows that.

But there's still another element to the Savior's tears. After all, we can't overlook the fairly obvious reality that Jesus knows what He is doing there. He knows why He delayed to let Lazarus "die" in the first place. He knows He is going to resuscitate Lazarus and bring him back to life. He knows that in just a few moments, Lazarus was going to be standing in front of everyone talking, joking, laughing, telling some amazing stories about what he's just experienced – and maybe getting a little annoyed Jesus called him back from gold streets to his sandals and stone hut.

So why cry for a friend separated by death when He is about to undo that separation? This is the side of John 11:35 that Christians must work to remember. Jesus was also weeping because so many of those around Him who claimed to believe in Him and His promises were demonstrating in their hopeless grief that they didn't really believe. Everything He had taught them, everything they were supposed to know, everything they said they believed about Him and the truth of eternity, everything they'd been told about the promise of life that never ends, everything that should have been preventing their deep sorrow and despondent agony, replacing it instead with hope-tempered tears over temporary separation – Jesus saw no indication of any of it. And so He wept.

I wonder when He looks at our funerals today, does He see hopelessness and despair? Does He see men and women who wear His name but find no relief in it? And if so, I wonder if He doesn't weep again, asking "What more could I have done to make them believe?"

WHEN THE BEGINNING ENDS
WHAT HAPPENS WHEN WE DIE?

Please don't misunderstand – I'm not suggesting that Christians find some way to neutralize our emotions or suspend human sentiments. It is natural and healthy to cry for loved ones we won't hold, hug, or talk to on earth anymore. But we cry as those with hope – knowing that it is only our selfishness that desires they be present in the body with us, rather than absent the body and present with the Lord. We are right to weep in those moments, to feel the hurt brought on by this curse of sin, and even to struggle to deal with the painful reality that we will make no more earthly memories with the one now separated from us. But don't weep – don't ever weep – for the life that is in the company of Almighty God.

The truth of funerals is that they represent finality – the end of a life. Honestly, that simply isn't biblical. What is biblical is the enduring truth that Jesus, the most reliable authority you will ever encounter, assured me that when you walk past my casket, I will be more alive at that precise moment than you have ever seen me, or than I have ever experienced before.

Christians should not conduct funerals that mask the reality of what is happening. We should hold going away parties permeated by an excitement of where our loved one is, and where we will soon be. If Christ's church made this its obvious objective and noticeable focus whenever it handled the sleep of physical death, I can assure you Jesus wouldn't be weeping, and the world would be watching.

SEVEN

THE SHADOW OF DEATH

For some reason I feel the need to reiterate that I could be wrong about all this. My understanding of what happens at the moment of our physical death could be the mere ramblings of a mind conned by what atheist Christopher Hitchens called the "siren song of Paradise and the dread of Hell."[1]

But that's exactly why I am writing this book from the authority of Scripture. I don't want this to be a competition of intellects between Hitchens and Heck. I'm well aware of who falls short in that contest. No, I want to write in such a way that pits the theories and assessments of men against the words of the Bible. If Heaven is not real, then the Bible is lying, the Spirit that supposedly inspired the Bible is fake, and Jesus was either the world's worst liar or a raging lunatic. Either way, He's totally unworthy of our worship.

But here's where my study has brought me. I believe that God is real, and that Jesus was the embodiment of God in the flesh. I believe what Jesus said was real, and that what the Spirit inspired is real. I believe that the Bible is a miraculous text that simply must be – for a multitude of reasons – divine in nature and substance. I trust it because I don't think there is anything more authoritative – not even a mind as well-respected as Christopher Hitchens.

Now, perhaps you know better. Maybe you've learned from someone smarter than the Author of Creation, someone whose reasoning is deeper than that of the Eternal God, someone whose logic is more sound than the Omnipotent. By all means, if that is the case, go with it. But allow me the courtesy of cautioning you: don't be wrong.

Several years ago in college, I remember staying up late one night to watch old episodes of the *Alfred Hitchcock Hour*. In one of them, I watched a man who had been sentenced to life in prison trying to execute an escape plan. He had befriended the jail's old undertaker – the old man himself a prisoner who suffered from serious medical problems. The lead character had schemed up a truly chilling idea that involved him slipping into the prison morgue at night, and hiding in the casket next to the dead body in the coffin. The undertaker would then come, and (with the assistance of the guards) he would wheel the casket out of the prison yard to the cemetery and bury it. The next morning, the plan went, he would return alone and dig the man out.

A few days later when the prison bells tolled signifying another prisoner death, the leading character put his plan into motion. That night he snuck down to the basement of the prison, and leaving all the lights off to avoid drawing attention, he crept over to the casket, raised the lid, climbed in next to the corpse, and pulled the lid down tight. Not long after, he felt the casket being loaded onto a cart and then wheeled out into the prison yard. He began to smile. And when he felt himself being lowered into the grave and dirt being shoveled on top of him, he could barely contain his excitement about the freedom that was now within his grasp.

But when morning came, the old man didn't show up. By afternoon, he began to panic and by evening he was frantically running out of air. Not knowing what else to do, he struck a match in the casket which provided just enough light to reveal that the face of the corpse was the face of the old man who had promised to dig him out. In planning for his freedom, he had made one fatal flaw. He had trusted in someone who himself was subject to the grave.

That's why I earnestly beg you, on this question about life beyond the grave, be overly cautious about who you trust and why. Because eternity is a long time to live with regrets. How long?

I'm always entertained when I hear human beings

WHEN THE BEGINNING ENDS
WHAT HAPPENS WHEN WE DIE?

attempt to wrap parameters of understanding around a concept like eternity. As beings bound by natural laws and limitations (like time), we are in an impossible position trying to explain or even comprehend concepts that exist beyond those laws (like eternity). But that doesn't seem to stop other people from trying, so why should it stop me?

Imagine yourself in line at Subway. There are 22 people in front of you. When each person gets up to order, they pull out a paper and say, "Okay, I'm going to need five different sandwiches." Every sandwich is toasted, foot long, with a full compliment of veggies. Every customer wants to pay by check. They each left their ID in the car. There's only one girl working that day. She's 15. It's her first day on the job. She doesn't speak English.

As comedian Emo Philips used to say, "You take a few minutes off that, and you begin to get an idea of how long eternity is."

No, I can't actually explain or articulate the duration of eternity, but I can say with certainty that its existence makes what happens on this side of the grave the all-important first note of a symphony. All-important because it determines whether the forthcoming concert will be divine or tragic, uplifting or heartbreaking, glorious or catastrophic.

From time to time, Jenny and I talk about what would happen if one of us were to die while we still have young children. Those conversations usually end with me telling her that our kids would need a good father figure in their life and if I die young, she needs to find someone to fill that role. She then tells me that I will do just fine without her if she dies young, and that if I find someone else she will haunt me for the rest of my life. Those kinds of conversations always get me thinking about the unimaginably difficult task of trying to explain a tragedy like that in a meaningful way to young kids.

Somehow, the late Dr. Donald Barnhouse did. Driving home from the funeral of his wife, Barnhouse recounts his difficulty in trying to make things make sense to his young children when he himself didn't fully understand. Even as an accomplished theologian, Barnhouse struggled to find the words until the moment he drove their car past a large semi truck on the highway. He asked his children if they noticed the shadow of the large truck that they just drove through. When the children all responded that they did, he asked them if they would prefer to be hit by the semi or be hit by its shadow. The children snickered as they stated the obvious: they'd much rather be hit by the shadow.

Barnhouse then taught this simple yet profound lesson. "When you die without Christ, you're hit by the semi. When you die with Christ, like Mom, you're hit by its shadow." The Psalmist affirms this profound reality writing, *Even though I walk through the valley of the **shadow** of death, I will fear no evil, for you are with* *me* (Psalm 23:4).

The position and teaching of Scripture is as clear as Dr. Tony Evans states it:

> "According to the Bible, if you are not a Christian, this life is the only Heaven you will ever know. But if you are a Christian, this life is the only Hell you will ever know."[2]

But how is that possible? Here's how: though our physical death is inevitable and unavoidable, God's love for us has found a way to remove the crushing weight of its blow. He's removed its sting. *Where, O death is your victory? Where, O death, is your sting?* (1 Corinthians 15:55)

Every time I read that passage I'm reminded of the story told by more ministers than I can count. While riding with his father in their family's old pick-up truck, a young boy is suddenly frightened by the presence of a large bee flying around the cab. As it zips back and forth around their heads and arms the boy ducks for cover and squeals in fear.

At that moment, the father reaches out his large hand and with a quick swiping motion captures the bee in the palm of his hand. He clinches his fist tight for a few seconds and then opens to let the bee fly out. The boy jumps back again and cowers by the door as the agitated bee starts circling even more aggressively than before.

The father speaks reassuringly to his scared boy, "Son, you don't have to worry – that bee can buzz and bluster, but it cannot sting you. See," he says, opening his red and slightly swollen palm, "I've got his stinger right here."[3]

On the cross at Calvary, our Father reached out and captured the hornet of death in the palm of His nail-scarred hands. Hands that now reach out to us, promising that we need not fear the sting of death any longer, for it has been once for all placed upon *the Lamb of God who takes away the sins of the world* (John 1:29) and nailed to a cross. He alone has taken away death's victory, meaning we can find victory over death in Him alone.

Anyone who thinks that I will one day be enjoying paradise because I contribute to charity, because I work to make a positive impact on the lives of young people, because I preach the gospel, because I go to church, because I'm a "good" guy, simply doesn't accept, believe, or understand the words of Scripture.

If we are going to trust the Bible is right about the existence of Heaven and Hell, then we must trust the Bible when it tells us how we get there.

If Jesus is not who He claimed to be, I am lost. If Jesus is not resurrected from the grave, I am still in my sins and the hornet still has its stinger.

If Jesus is not in Heaven, I can't go. But if He is there, I won't miss it for anything this world can offer.

EIGHT

GOD UNDERSTANDS RESERVATIONS

I had my Seinfeld moment not long ago. To be fair, any fan of that iconic NBC television sitcom will tell you one of the most charming things about it was how often it reflected the real experiences of real people. For those like me who get somewhat annoyed with programs that attempt to portray an existential crisis of epic proportions…and then resolve it in 25 minutes, Seinfeld was a hit.

They made entire episodes about the minutia of daily life. And that's why when something happens to you and the person next to you asks, "Did you watch Seinfeld?" it's because they are about to reference a moment in the show that directly corresponds to your very predicament. And that very thing happened to me just a few months ago.

I had rented a car from the rental giant Avis for an out-of-state speaking trip I had that weekend. I had reserved an economy-size car that would get much better gas mileage than my Jeep, and that would be more reliable to travel long distances. I had paid for my reservation online. When the day of the pick-up came around, I pulled into the Avis lot and noticed there were only two cars there – neither an economy size. Nevertheless, I strolled in confidently, knowing that I had a reservation (I'd even taken the printed copy of the reservation so there could be no question).

The girl behind the desk look terrified and completely overwhelmed the moment I walked through the door. It was fairly obvious she wasn't very educated, and on top of that she quickly informed me it was her first day on the job. When I told her I had a reservation and showed her my receipt, she looked at me blankly and said, "We don't have any more cars except that luxury one out there. You want that?" I said, "Well, I really wanted one that got good gas mileage, but if that's all you got, I guess I don't really have a choice." She said, "Okay, it will be an additional $150."

What?

My response was far more of a kneejerk reaction than what I should have allowed. I retorted with a laugh, "I don't think so." When she just stared at me, clearly concerned about this confrontation she did

WHEN THE BEGINNING ENDS
WHAT HAPPENS WHEN WE DIE?

not want to have on her first day, I backed down and said, "Okay, listen, I know this isn't your fault, but since this is your company's mistake, you really should upgrade me at no additional cost. Your competitors do that." She said, "Sir, I don't think that's our policy, but I'll get my manager on the phone."

And what ensued with the manager was straight out of Seinfeld:

> Manager: Oh I'm sorry we have no mid-size available at the moment.
>
> Jerry: I don't understand, I made a reservation. Do you have my reservation?
>
> Manager: Yes, we do. Unfortunately we ran out of cars.
>
> Jerry: But the reservation keeps the car here. That's why you have the reservation.
>
> Manager: I know why we have reservations.
>
> Jerry: I don't think ya do. If ya did, I'd have a car. See, you know how to take the reservation, you just don't know how to hold the

reservation. And that's really the most important part of the reservation – the holding.[1]

You can ask my wife, it's been a long time since I've been that frustrated. As you might guess:

(1) Avis wouldn't budge
(2) Neither would I
(3) I drove my Jeep that weekend out of state

Even if you've never dealt with the false guarantee of a rental car company, every one of us knows the feeling of being led to believe something that isn't true – empty promises and broken pledges. If not for those things, politicians wouldn't know what to do with themselves. And I say that in the truest spirit of bipartisanship.

From Republican Nixon's promise that he wasn't a crook to Democrat Bill Clinton's promise he didn't have sexual relations with that woman; from Republican George H.W. Bush's, "Read my lips, no new taxes" pledge to Democrat Barack Obama's, "If you like your doctor, you can keep your doctor" pledge, it seems that those with the most authority over our lives are also the least honest about it.

So amidst all the deceit, what makes me so confident about this place called Heaven? Precisely because of what this world has taught me about promises – they are only as good and reliable as the one who is making them. With that in mind, check out what Jesus says:

> *Do not let your hearts be troubled. You believe in God; believe also in Me. My Father's house has many rooms; if that were not so, would I have told you that I am going there to prepare a place for you? And if I go and prepare a place for you, I will come back and take you to be with me that you also may be where I am* (John 14:1-3).

In this one passage, Jesus connects the promise of heaven to the:

(1) Character of God
(2) Character of Christ
(3) Character of Scripture (inspired by the Spirit)

In other words, if Heaven is not real, each of them are liars and untrustworthy. If you believe that, then why are you still reading this book? I confessed from the first pages of this text that I begin with the assumption of the Bible's veracity. Some people say, "Man, that takes a lot of faith." Actually, it doesn't.

In Old Testament days, when Moses or Abraham exhibited faith and confidence in the promises of God, they were reassured both by His blessing and His personal, sometimes verbal interaction with them. In the New Testament era, God wasn't communicating in the same way with His creation, which is why Jesus says to His disciples, *Believe also in Me* (John 14:1). He's telling them, "I'm God in the flesh – so if believing in a God you can't see is too hard for you, you know Me. You've seen what I do and know who I am. And I am telling you that this promise of eternal paradise is true."

And now in our day, we don't have God speaking to us through burning bushes or Jesus chilling with us around a campfire. But we have two unique, miraculous reassurances.

First, we have the testimony, truth, and compiled Word of God *once for all delivered to the saints* (Jude 1:3). Repeatedly throughout Scripture we see the promise of Heaven reiterated to us. In Philippians, Paul reminds us that *our citizenship is in heaven. And we eagerly await a Savior from there, the Lord Jesus Christ* (3:20).

Second, we have the indwelling of God Himself in the form of the Holy Spirit. Remember that shortly before Jesus ascended to Heaven after the resurrection, His disciples worried about how they will know where to go, what to do, how to act, who to talk to, and when to do it all. Jesus tells them something profound:

> *But very truly I tell you, it is for your good that I am going away. Unless I go away, the Holy Spirit will not come to you; but if I go, I will send him to you* (John 16:7).

Did you catch that? Jesus tells His disciples that it is *better* for them that He is leaving. Why? Because Jesus in physical form could be in one place at a time. If He's talking with Peter, He can't be inspiring and protecting James. But the Holy Spirit would be the helper, advocate, and counselor sent to each of His followers offering strength, wisdom, guidance, and truth when called upon.

And though it is certainly a subjective experience relative to each believer how they encounter and move with the Spirit, it is an objective reality that every believer knows the indwelling of that Spirit. He is real, He is alive, and He is active.

Why do I believe in the promise of Heaven? Because the Bible – the Word of God, embodied in Jesus, inspired by the Spirit – tells me so.

NINE

IMAGINING THE UNIMAGINABLE

So according to the Bible, what is this Heaven all about? Who will we see? What will we experience? Before we dive into this, I think it's important to issue a disclaimer. Answering questions about what Heaven is like, even with the Bible as our guide, is extremely difficult. As created humans, we think and speak within the boundaries of finite terms. But heaven is a place consumed with the infinite:

- Infinite grace
- Infinite beauty
- Infinite duration
- Infinite joy
- Infinite contentment

Consider that even Biblical authors inspired by the Spirit, and even those who themselves *saw* or experienced Heaven found it difficult to express in human terms. The prophet Ezekiel describes whirlwinds, a cloud of fire engulfing itself, unworldly brightness radiating outward, four living creatures with the appearance of a man (Ezekiel 1:4-14).

Paul, speaking of his own experience, actually admitted it's not even possible to describe:

> *I know a man in Christ who fourteen years ago was caught up to the third heaven. Whether it was in the body or out of the body I do not know – God knows. And I know that this man – whether in the body or apart from the body I do not know, but God knows – was caught up to Paradise and heard inexpressible things, things that no one is permitted to tell* (2 Corinthians 12:2-4).

By the way, don't let Paul's reference to the "third Heaven" confuse you. The first "heaven" is a reference to the sky we see, the second "heaven" is what we call space, and the third "Heaven" is what we know as "Heaven."

After reading this passage, you can hopefully see the dilemma we face when someone asks us to tell them what Heaven is like. Humans who have seen it and actually been there can't even find the words to begin to describe it. The dwelling place of God is in every sense inexpressible. King Solomon noted that himself as he attempted to construct God's temple on earth:

> But will God really dwell on earth? The heavens, even the highest Heaven, cannot contain you. How much less this temple I have built (1 Kings 8:27)!

Wait a minute. Did you see what Solomon's inspired words just told us about God? The "heavens" – in this context meaning the entire universe – can't even contain God. Before we go any further, stop to consider the sizes that we're talking about here. Writing at *Wired Magazine*, reporter Adam Mann tries to encapsulate it this way:

> Space, as Douglas Adams once so aptly wrote, is big.
>
> To try imagining how big, place a penny down in front of you. If our sun were the size of that penny, the nearest star, Alpha Centauri, would be 350 miles away. Depending on where you live, that's very likely in the next state (or possibly country) over.
>
> Attempting to imagine distances larger than this quickly becomes troublesome. At this scale, the Milky Way galaxy would be 7.5 million miles across, or more than 30 times the distance between the Earth and the moon. As you can see, these are rather inhuman

dimensions that are almost impossible to really get a sense of.[1]

The scale and size we're talking about is just mind numbing, and yet we also know that the universe is expanding every moment. Still, Solomon says even that is far too small to encapsulate God. God is bigger than everything He created. But somehow we want to try to wrap our puny minds around His eternal kingdom of Paradise. Good luck with that.

But just when we think it's a lost cause to try to understand, God does what He always seems to do for us. He reaches out to help us. In the book of Revelation, God gives the disciple John a vision, not of Heaven in full – otherwise John would have undoubtedly been in the same confused and dumbstruck state that Paul and Ezekiel found themselves. No, God shows John something *coming down from heaven* (Revelation 21:10).

God takes from Heaven something we can understand, a city, and puts it before John to describe for us. He writes,

> *And He carried me away in the spirit to a mountain great and high, and showed me the Holy City, Jerusalem, coming down out of Heaven from God. It shone with the glory of God, and its brilliance was like that of a very precious jewel, like a jasper, clear as crystal* (Revelation 21:10-11).

This isn't all of Heaven. John is taken to a mountain there and shown the capital city called the New Jerusalem. And between this vision and the conversation Jesus has with His disciples before leaving earth, we get a fascinating glimpse of what we can expect Heaven to be like.

One last reminder before we begin to unpack it, however, is in order. I had never been to the Grand Canyon until I was in my mid 20s. I had heard descriptions of it, watch videos that showed it, and even looked at my grandparents' photos from their trip there. My Granny missed her calling as a Japanese tourist – the woman took rolls and rolls of film on their trip there.

So when my college roommate and I were taking our wild west spring break trip a few years after graduation – a journey where we drove from our Indiana homes to the Pacific Ocean, touched it and then drove back – and we decided to stop briefly at the Grand Canyon on our way home, I knew precisely what I thought I would see.

I remember driving up to one of the overlooks. The road curved towards a parking lot, and as I glanced out my window to make sure I was clear of oncoming traffic before making my turn, my eyes saw it for the first time. I am not joking, my knees went weak at that very moment. Had I been standing, I probably would have stumbled a bit. I remember just saying, "Holy cow," as Syd turned around to see it himself. When I walked up to it, that feeling returned to my knees but I was at least prepared for it. The one thing I will never forget about that experience was how poor of a representation all the videos – even those done with the most exquisite camera work – all of the photos, and all the descriptions had offered of this canyon masterpiece.

What I'm about to do in the following pages, is the equivalent of trying to describe the Grand Canyon for you. I am going to be explaining what Scripture expresses about what we will see, do, and know in Heaven, doing my best to paint a picture of it in your mind.

My description will be woefully short of its reality. But that's all I can possibly do. That and assure you one day your knees will go weak.

TEN

WHAT WE WILL SEE

When John begins recording what he saw coming down out of Heaven, he uses an extremely appropriate analogy:

> Then I saw 'a new Heaven and a new Earth.' For the first Heaven and the first Earth had passed away, and there was no longer any sea. I saw the holy city, the New Jerusalem, coming down out of Heaven from God, prepared as a bride beautifully dressed for her husband (Revelation 21:1-2).

Recently, some friends of mine were planning their wedding and discussing whether or not they should see each other for pictures before the service, or abide by the increasingly rare tradition of the groom seeing his bride in her gown for the first time when she's walking down the aisle. They asked what we thought, and when Jenny responded that she and I had seen each other for pictures before the service, the couple's jaws dropped.

"You mean, he saw you before the service, and he *still* reacted like that when the doors opened?"

Yes, yes I did. Apparently, from what I understand, I was a tad bit emotional at our wedding. I say "from what I understand" because that whole day is a bit of a blur to me. I do remember sitting alone in a separate room shortly before the service, opening a card and small present from my soon-to-be-wife. I melted. And after that, I just don't remember much.

Frankly I think many of the stories surrounding my overly sensitive reaction have taken on a bit of tall-tale exaggeration through the years. But I do remember at the moment Jenny came down the aisle feeling an overwhelming wave of emotions. I wasn't alone though – as I recall, everyone who saw her that day let out a collective gasp. She looked incredible. Having that personal experience, it makes John's analogy in Revelation very appropriate.

Our first glimpse of Heaven will elicit nothing short of gasps of amazement and wonder at the breathtaking beauty. I have never been in the presence of a believer as they depart this world for the next. But when a dear friend of mine and faithful servant of Christ died a few years ago in the presence of his family they told me his final words were repeating, "Oh wow. Wow. Oh my."

I have no way of knowing for certain what was happening to him at that moment. Perhaps it was nothing but the random firing of synapses in his brain that atheist scientists suggest cause us to believe we are walking towards brilliant light. Maybe he was having a dream. Maybe his family misheard what they wanted to hear from unintelligible words. Certainly not everyone who dies has that same experience or says similar things. But many do. And it sounds a tremendous amount like what one might say seeing a bride beautifully prepared for her husband on their wedding day.

John offers more than just analogy in this passage, thankfully. He describes the actual dimensions of this city:

> *The city was laid out like a square, as long as it was wide. He measured the city with the rod and found it to be 12,000 stadia in length, and as wide and high as it is long. The angel measured the wall using human measurement, and it was 144 cubits thick. The wall was made of jasper, and the city of pure gold, as pure as glass. The foundations of the city walls were decorated with every kind of precious stone. The first foundation was jasper, the*

second sapphire, the third agate, the fourth emerald, the fifth onyx, the sixth ruby, the seventh chrysolite, the eighth beryl, the ninth topaz, the tenth turquoise, the eleventh jacinth, and the twelfth amethyst. The twelve gates were twelve pearls, each gate made of a single pearl. The great street of the city was of gold, as pure as transparent glass (Revelation 21:16-21).

To be honest, I've always just glossed over that passage. It would usually go like this in my mind: "The city was laid out like a square, as long as it is wide. He measured the city, a bunch of weird angles, and lengths, walls are cool metals and jewels and stuff, blah, blah, 12 gates, streets in the city are gold, they're transparent, yeah, yeah." I don't say that to be rude, but unless you're really investigating what Heaven is like, you're just inclined to skim right past dimensions and stone types. Before I let you criticize me for that, how about you get out the graph paper and chart out the dimensions of Noah's Ark or the Bronze Altar of Israel from memory. That's my point — we typically skim specifics like this passage offers.

But this time actually pay attention to what this extremely descript account from John is telling us about Heaven, because it's absolutely fascinating.

- The city is laid out like a box. It is as long as it is wide as it is tall.

- That introduces a captivating thought – there are layers to this city.
- The size of this one city is astounding. It is as long as the distance between New York City and Denver. It as wide as the distance between the U.S. border with Canada and the U.S. border with Mexico. That's just one city.
- And remember that's just one layer of the city. Continue stacking those layers on top of each other as tall as that same distance (NYC-Denver).
- This is a city that alone could be home to billions of people.
- The city's walls, roads, streets and infrastructure appear to be composed of the most precious and rare jewels and stones.
- These stones and precious metals are so pure and refined, unlike anything we have seen, that they take on a transparent quality, allowing us to look through them and beyond them.

From this description alone, it's almost as though looking at the entire city from the outside would give it the appearance of a massive jewel, sparkling, glittering, and exuding unimaginable brilliance.

Now, couple this with what we read in Isaiah:

> *In the year that King Uzziah died, I saw the Lord, high and exalted seated on a throne; and the train of His robe filled the temple. Above Him were the Seraphim, each with six wings: with two wings they covered their faces, with two they covered their*

feet, and with two they were flying. And they were calling to one another: 'Holy, Holy, Holy, is the Lord Almighty: the whole earth is full of His glory' (Isaiah 6:1-3).

Look at that last line and consider its implications. *The whole earth is full of His glory* (Isaiah 6:3). Heaven will be full of God. His all-consuming presence will be everywhere – over everything, through everything, in everything. Often times you will hear people comment about the beauty God has created here on earth. They will point to open skies, comment on Instagram photos of sunsets, or marvel at the changing leaves, and remark on God's handiwork.

But remember in each of those examples God's beauty remains inhibited by the presence of sin on earth. No matter how gorgeous of a sky God paints for us, on earth we can never fully appreciate it because of the filter of sin that saturates us. In Heaven, that filter is removed. In Heaven, God doesn't need the sun or the moon as His agents of illumination – He Himself is the light.

And according to John, He has created His cities as transparent jewels, each carefully designed to reflect and refract His brilliance in every direction, into every corner, into every space, in every moment.

This is just a glimpse of what our eyes – that will never have to close in sleep or rest – will see in God's Paradise.

ELEVEN

WHAT WE WILL DO

It was a Saturday night at the Heck house and we had just finished our bedtime Bible story with the kids – for some reason Grayson is really into the plague of the boils that God brought upon Egypt. Disconcerting? No question.

But after I read to them, we all close our eyes and say our bedtime prayer together. That night I prayed for a good morning at church the next day, and when I said "Amen," Addie piped up and asked me, "Why do we go to church?"

In my head I started working through my theologically profound answer of the importance of not giving up the habit of coming together on the first day of the week as the early church had committed itself to, in order remember the death, burial, and resurrection of Jesus from the grave (Acts

2:42). I think Jenny could tell I was going to overcomplicate things, and so she jumped in, "Church is God's house and so we go to be with Him."

"Oh," Addie said. "I like going to church." They scurried off to bed before I was even able to give my opening statement. Bummer.

For those like my children who (thankfully) enjoy the weekly reunion that is church on earth, Heaven is going to be right up their alley:

> *And I heard a loud voice from the throne saying, 'Look! God's dwelling place is now among the people, and He will dwell with them, they will be His people, and God Himself will be with them and be their God'* (Revelation 21:3).

If church is "God's house and we go to be with Him," then Heaven is one gigantic, never-ending church service. Now, if you aren't like my kids and church isn't one of your favorite things, that might give you pause. For still others of you, those who loathe church services for one reason or another, you might even shutter at the thought of this. How can it be Heaven if it is anything like dragging myself to that boring church building every Sunday morning? If that's your attitude, let's first establish that your attitude stinks. But I still have some good news for you.

Our concept of worship is pretty flawed, Biblically

speaking. After all, whenever someone talks about worship, they are usually talking about singing hymns or praise songs. When churches hire a worship minister, they are usually defining that role as the person who, among a handful of other responsibilities, leads the congregation in singing during services. And there's no question that singing praises to God is worship.

The problem is, we don't seem to grasp the rest of what worship is. Worship is when you get together with friends and have supper. Worship is when you go out with the boys to play pick-up basketball. Worship is laughing and talking with your spouse in the car. Worship is when you go to work. *Everything we do as believers, according to Scripture, is to be done for the glory of God* (1 Corinthians 1:31). It is our *spiritual act of worship* (Romans 12:1) to be living sacrifices, holy and pleasing to God at all times – not just in the church building.

As Christians, God is supposed to animate all our conversations, all our interactions, all our exchanges, all our conduct – not just our 20-minute emotional experience singing songs with dramatic key changes and orchestral swells. To the degree we've lost sight of that, we fail to comprehend what worship is, and thus confuse this amazing promise of Heaven in Revelation for some uninspiring guarantee that our eternity is to be filled with "church."

Dr. Evans writes,

WHEN THE BEGINNING ENDS
WHAT HAPPENS WHEN WE DIE?

"The city (that John sees, the New Jerusalem) is the sanctuary; so everything we do, everywhere we go, every conversation will be worship because it will encompass all of life. Every second of every day will be sheer ecstasy and joy. There will never be a time when God feels distant, or silent, or disconnected. You will be high on God all the time."[1]

I've been privileged to speak at a lot of church camps and summer youth conferences. And a recurring theme at every single one of those is how to help students guard against the "spiritual high" they experience, only to have it come crashing back to earth after they've been home for a week.

Even as an adult, it still happens to me. I will speak at a conference, watch kids make life-changing, eternity-altering decisions, be surrounded by incredible musicians who lead and prompt spiritual experiences in the main services, and be fully devoted and completely consumed in godly things for a week. Then I go home, and after the initial excitement of seeing my family, I have a let down. Paying the bills, fixing cement cracks in the sidewalk, settling arguments with warring preschoolers at home – as joyous as those experiences can be, they aren't quite the spiritual equivalent.

What Evans is affirming is that the spiritual high of Heaven will never wear off. And lest you believe that being on a "high" all the time would wear you out, remember you won't be dealing with this earthly body.

> *Dear friends, now we are children of God, and what we will be has not yet been made known. But we know that when Christ appears, we shall be like Him, for we shall see Him as He is* (1 John 3:2).

That promise *we shall be like Him* tells us a great deal about our resurrected bodies. We will function physically like the resurrected body of Jesus did. If you remember, Jesus walked through doors, passed through clouds, and while He was able to enjoy the benefits of earthly life like eating, He didn't have to do it for nourishment. The supernatural bodies we receive in Heaven are reiterations of our earthly bodies but as God intended them to be – that is, apart from sin and its effects: glorified, eternal, perfect, and incapable of growing weary.

And since they are perfected versions of our physical, earthly bodies, we will be recognizable and known. When people foolishly lament that "we won't know people" in Heaven like we know them here on earth, they are failing to acknowledge the testimony of Scripture. Remember this account after the resurrection of Jesus:

WHEN THE BEGINNING ENDS
WHAT HAPPENS WHEN WE DIE?

> *Jesus said to her, 'Mary.' She turned toward Him and cried out in Aramaic, 'Teacher!'* (John 20:16)

This was the resurrected body of Jesus, yet it still looked like Him. Mary knew Him. And shortly after that encounter, Jesus appeared to two of His disciples on the road to Emmaus (Luke 24:1-35). After intentionally disguising Himself, He allows the eyes of His disciples to be opened and they immediately recognize Him.

If we are assured in First John that *we shall be like Him* (3:2), we too will be our recognizable selves. There's additional evidence of this reality back when Jesus was transfigured on the mountain. There, two heavenly forms appeared with Him. And Peter, who had been accompanying Jesus, knew who they were:

> *Peter said to Jesus, 'Lord it is good for us to be here. If you wish, I will put up three shelters – one for you, one for Moses and one for Elijah'* (Matthew 17:4).

So here's what we know about our appearances in Heaven. You will be you and I will be me, keeping our races and cultures, but seeing them glorified in the perfect "one race" perspective that God always intended. We will participate in an eternity of kingdoms and nations of men (Revelation 21:24, 26) but our flaws, imperfections, and weaknesses will be totally eliminated.

There's a tendency to think only about the lack of disease, physical pain, and effects of aging when we talk about these perfected bodies of Heaven. But since Heaven is the complete removal of the curse, we will be reaching our full potential as image-bearers of the Creator. And that means our minds and mental capacity are going to be perfected as well.

My whole life I've heard people talk about the untapped potential of the human intellect. But it was not until I spoke alongside famed neurosurgeon Dr. Ben Carson at a banquet that I was able to understand just how powerful the mind could be if fully unleashed.

When Dr. Carson spoke these words, I was so blown away by them I jotted them down immediately. He said, "I've worked on the brain my whole life, and it's amazing. If you learned one new thing every second, it would take you 3 million years to challenge the capacity of the human brain." Obviously I have no way to verify or validate that claim, but I have no reason to doubt the award-winning former head of neurosurgery at Johns Hopkins. And as I said, Carson is far from the only brain scientist to make this assessment. We've all heard countless other academics talk about the untouched richness of the human brain. What is it truly capable of comprehending, understanding, and grasping? One day we will know.

For now we see only a reflection as in a

WHEN THE BEGINNING ENDS
WHAT HAPPENS WHEN WE DIE?

mirror; then we shall see face to face. Now I know in part; then I shall know fully, even as I am fully known (1 Corinthians 13:12).

On earth, just like everything else, our brains are hampered and hindered as a result of Adam's fall in Genesis 3. Unencumbered by those earthly realities in Heaven, however, we will learn and retain the secrets of God Himself. We will know *fully*. Every second will bring the excitement of learning something new, never to be forgotten, confused, or mistaken.

In what is surely my version of the "We had to walk 10 miles to school uphill both ways" old person lecture, I often complain to my high school students that I went to college in the era where the Internet was in its infancy. While chat rooms, email, and search engines were just cutting their teeth, I was driving across the state to visit university libraries in a desperate attempt to find research sources on the women's suffrage movement for my senior seminar paper. I can't imagine the ease of writing such a complex paper by merely clicking through the parsed and filtered content produced by a Google search today.

I know that's an incredibly impotent analogy to describe something as overwhelming as having instantaneous access to the knowledge of God, but it still offers a layman's understanding of the speed and ease with which we will one day learn and process everything we've ever wanted to know – and things we didn't even know we wanted to know.

So again, don't talk to me about how you worry Heaven might be boring. You won't have time to be bored, because you will be learning and understanding every time you turn around. And this amazing, astounding reality will continue in perpetuity. How can I know? Because even with an eternity at our disposal, we will never come close to exhausting the mind of a God whose own universe can't even contain Him.

TWELVE

HOW WE WILL FEEL

One of the more interesting parts of being a teacher is to see how quickly new students acclimate and adjust to the culture around them. For the most part, you can always tell right away when the new kid is outgoing and self-confident, or when they are shy and uneasy. I feel a little bit sorry for the latter group, mainly because I don't really remember ever feeling that way.

Call it middle child syndrome or whatever, but in the few times my family moved to a new school, or even when I went off to college, there wasn't much in the way of fear or trepidation for me – at least not that I have any real recollection of experiencing. But I know that for so many others, the feeling of dread that comes upon them when they are being thrust into a new situation, with new surroundings, new peers, and a new culture, is all too real.

He never opened up to me about it, but I feel pretty confident in saying that apprehension and angst was exactly what my older brother Andrew experienced time and again growing up. Even after having adjusted to college, and even having moved on to law school, he was always so much happier if he could be home with our family in a comfortable environment. That isn't to imply that I wasn't happier with my family than with strangers, but just that leaving familiarity didn't cause me nearly the anxiety that it did him.

In reading the Scriptures, it is quite clear that regardless of whether you're more like Andrew or you're more like me, Heaven is not going to require any form of an adjustment period. Look how Jesus describes it:

> *My Father's house has many rooms; if that were not so, would I have told you that I am going there to prepare a place for you? And if I go and prepare a place for you, I will come back and take you to be with me that you also may be where I am* (John 14:1-3).

One of the most attractive parts of Heaven has nothing to do with the incredible sights we will behold. It has everything to do with the exceeding familiarity of every person we encounter, every interaction we have, every meeting we experience. The colloquial terminology we use for our fellow

WHEN THE BEGINNING ENDS
WHAT HAPPENS WHEN WE DIE?

Christians here on earth, referring to one another as "brother" and "sister," will take on a dimension of unsurpassed reality once we enter Heaven. I hate to use this description only because I don't know many people that actually enjoy going to these, but what we are set to experience in Heaven is the most perfect family reunion imaginable.

Look at how Jesus describes this as His "Father's house." That's quite intentionally a very personal description that I think we can all wrap our minds around with one of two analogies.

One of my favorite feelings in the world is coming home after a long vacation. Jenny is always adamant before we leave that we change the sheets on the bed, sweep the floors, and have the house as spotless as it can be. And even though I always drag my feet about it at the time, making wise cracks to the kids about how we want to make sure that the burglars are able to find everything in a timely manner and not have any obstacles as they are carrying out all our valuables (for some reason Jenny never finds the humor in that), I have to admit that when we get back I am so glad she insisted on doing it.

Being able to walk in, drop the bags, shower in my own shower, climb into my own bed, turn on my own TV, and sleep on my own pillow, even after having been in a nice hotel or resort for a week, is one of the greatest feelings in the world. The familiarity of home is unsurpassed.

Scripture constantly refers to believers in this world as strangers (1 Peter 2:11-12) – citizens of Heaven (Philippians 3:20) whose homeland is in another time and place (Colossians 3:15-17). Tortured as this may make the text, consider this life an 80-year vacation, playing, working, and living far away from home. What Jesus promises here is that when this vacation ends, the familiarity we will experience when we walk through the gates, drop our bags, and head to our rooms will be the greatest feeling of home we've ever experienced.

The other way we could explain this actually doesn't work for me, but it might for you. My wife and I live so close to both our parents that we don't ever really "come home" for the holidays or for a visit. We're always here. But for those who do make an annual or bi-annual trek back to their childhood homes, this can be a powerful analogy. There's a charming comfort and contentment for people when they return to their "home" after years of living elsewhere. The memories, the late night conversations, the reminiscing – none of it feels strange or unknown. It feels like home.

Jenny and I always notice her mom's preparations every time her oldest son (Jenny's big brother) and his family come from states away for Thanksgiving. She buys their favorite foods, she hangs new drapes in their room, she gets the kind of candy they like for the bowls, and has all their favorite movies and kid toys clean and ready. She isn't preparing for a houseguest. She's preparing for family.

Jesus makes it very clear in this passage that He isn't preparing for a massive influx of houseguests or visitors. He and the Father are preparing for family to come home. And if you think your earthly mom and dad know you and your interests well, just wait. Remember God created you, knit you together (Psalm 139:13) – that includes not just your physical form, but your emotions, personality, temperament, and dispositions.

Another way of saying that is that He knows us better than we know ourselves (Romans 8:27-37). Which means He knows what we like more than we do. In fact, He knows things we will like that we've never even imagined before. That's why when I've heard some preachers liken the preparation in Heaven to what first-time parents prepare in their baby's nursery, I think the comparison falls flat.

Yes, ultrasounds reveal the sex of the baby about to be born. That allows the soon-to-be Mom and Dad to adorn the nursery with either princesses or footballs. But not every girl likes princesses. My girls do, but my wife never did. Not every boy likes football. Some are far more interested in tractors or trains or racecars. When you prepare a nursery for a newborn, you are doing so generically – blue for boys, pink for girls. That's not what God is doing. God is preparing our rooms with our tastes, preferences, and personalities at the heart of His work.

Every so often I look back through my collection of cards that I've received from my wife through the years. And when I do, I find myself glossing over the printed words of Hallmark and skipping right down to the handwritten notes or poems that Jen wrote to me personally. That's what Jesus is getting at – what God has waiting for us isn't the scripted verse of a poet that can be applied to thousands of different relationships. It's a handwritten love letter, full of inside jokes, memories only you share, and meant for you and you alone.

Speaking of intimate relationships, one of the questions I've always wondered about the most is how well we will know each other in Heaven. Will I know my earthly neighbor when I see him there? Will I know my college professor, my uncle, or the babysitter from my childhood? How about instead of just saying "yes," I take it a step further and suggest that you don't know them at all compared to how you will know them once you're there.

To illustrate this, Dr. Evans uses the common exchange many of us have with colleagues, friends, and acquaintances on a daily basis. We say, "How are you?" but we don't really mean it. It's just what you say in conversation. And they answer back, "Doing fine," but they don't really mean it either. Maybe they're going through a divorce, the sickness of a child, the loss of a parent, financial concerns, a bout with an anxiety disorder, or a million other things that make them not "fine." But that's what they say because that's what we're trained to say. After all, who asks, "How are you?" to a co-worker and desires a full 20-minute explanation of everything going on in their heart and mind?

But here's the thing about Heaven – there are no facades, no pretenses, no walls. In Heaven we are revealed for who we truly are; the living embodiment of everything God created us to be. Outside of my wife, few people see the real me. And even though we say we keep no secrets from our spouses, there are inevitably things we struggle with, issues we deal with, and traits we keep hidden from even those closest to us. We do it because our earthly shame or sensitivity demands we pull a mask over our weaknesses in an effort to be who we are supposed to be and want to be. In Heaven, we *are* that person and everyone will know it. They will know us.

I feel confident in reading Scripture that I will know George Washington if he's there. I feel confident in reading Scripture that I will know my great grandma. I feel confident in reading Scripture that I will know all of my earthly family members who have gone on before me. Remember in the tragic account of King David's sin with Bathsheba that he loses his young son as a result of his wickedness. After being informed of his son's death, David ceases his fasting and prayer, worships God and eats for the first time in weeks. Seeing this dramatic change, some of those around him asked him to account for his behavior and David responds by saying,

> *While the child was still alive, I fasted and wept. I thought, 'Who knows? The LORD may be gracious to me and let the child live.' But now that he is dead, why should I go on fasting? Can I bring him back again? I will go to him, but he will not return to me* (2 Samuel 12: 22-23).

Notice that last line says *I will go to him.* There's an implication there that shouldn't be overlooked. David does not say that he will never see his son again, or even that he will merely share an eternity in the same place. He specifically says that when he goes to Heaven, he will go to "him," his son. That makes no sense if David won't know his son there.

But again, the miraculous, almost unimaginable thing about Heaven is that everyone we encounter even if not "familiar" to us like our earthly children, will be "familial" to us. They will be our family and we will be their family. Including even the great saints:

> *But you have come to Mount Zion, to the city of the living God, the heavenly Jerusalem. You have come to thousands upon thousands of angels in joyful assembly, to the church of the firstborn, whose names are written in heaven. You have come to God, the Judge of all, to the spirits of the righteous made perfect, to Jesus the mediator of a new covenant, and to the sprinkled blood that speaks a*

better word than the blood of Abel (Hebrews 12:22-24).

This excites me beyond words – I will be able to talk with John the Baptist as a brother. You will be able to hear from your brother Moses what was going through his mind the moment the blood poured from his staff and filled the Nile River, we will all get to sit around a table and be regaled by Noah's stories about disposing of that much animal waste on the Ark. And I'm sure several of her sisters will be talking to Eve often about how much they enjoyed the labor pains she initiated with her choices (I know Scripture says that painful memories will be wiped from our minds, but I was in that delivery room and if any memory can make it through the heavenly barrier my money's on that one).

These encounters, relationships, and conversations will come to be part of our daily routine as we go about our work in Heaven.

And if that word "work" confuses you, recognize that is part of the familiarity of Heaven. Life there seems to embody similarity to life here – jobs to do, work to complete, people to talk with, places to visit – but all of it done in a perfect environment, without the toil of labor and without the temptation of sin. Remember God's very nature is that of a worker (John 5:17) and His plan from the beginning of creation was to place man in a perfect environment to do work:

The LORD God took the man and put him in the Garden of Eden to work it and take care of it (Genesis 2:15).

For most people on earth there is a drudgery or toil associated with their life's occupation. Whether it's the monotony of factory work, the long hours of the law office, the paperwork of an office job, the teenage attitudes of teaching, the early mornings of a paper route, there's something we can find to complain about in nearly every job we do here. Nearly, but I don't think all.

Several years ago I started a project to remake our backyard into a tropical oasis. Yes, in central Indiana. It's involved 200 tons of fill dirt, mound building, fence moving, deck construction, plumbing for waterfalls, ponds, spitting tiki-men, and mini-geysers, rock moving, tree planting, wiring for speakers, hanging lights, and much more. We are very blessed, but certainly not in a position to pay for this kind of an overhaul to be done by professionals, so I've endeavored to do it myself. That surprises a lot of people mainly because I don't come across as the outdoorsman type. Most people expect to see me behind a computer or at a desk as opposed to standing knee deep in a trench with PVC pipe all around me. But I love it.

In fact, I love it so much that I've only had two major complaints about it to this point: I wish I had more money, and I wish I had more time. In the late spring or early fall, I will find myself staring out the window at work sometimes just aching to get home and get started on it. When it rains I'm depressed that I can't be out there working.

And I'm sure I'm not alone in this kind of obsession. Most people have a hobby or work that they give themselves that they truly enjoy. Whether it's redecorating a room, re-doing a kitchen, souping-up a car, or scrapbooking, there is work we love to do and can't wait to get back to. That's what is in store for us in Heaven. Randy Alcorn writes it this way:

> We'll also have work to do, satisfying and enriching work that we can't wait to get back to, work that'll never be drudgery. God is the primary worker, and as His image-bearers, we're made to work. We create, accomplish, set goals and fulfill them—to God's glory.[1]

You will reach your full potential in Heaven, every day, without failure, without frustration. You will work to God's glory never sensing a feeling of exasperation, never wishing you had more time, never second guessing your performance. Separated from your sin nature for eternity, you will find perfect fulfillment and purpose serving God and your heavenly family forever.

THIRTEEN

WHAT ABOUT OUR SPOUSE?

Sometimes it freaks me out how much I can be like the Pharisees and Sadducees described in the Bible. I'm a traditionalist and a conservative by nature, and therefore have Pharisaical tendencies that I have to guard against. I'm also a skeptic that doesn't go along with the next trend, movement, or theory just because the culture around me seems mesmerized by it. The Sadducees were like that in Jesus' day. So much so they were simply incredulous about the idea of an afterlife, and often tried to find stumping questions to pose to Jesus as a way of discrediting what they believed to be His absurd promise of some distant, eternal paradise.

One of their most popular questions is one that many Christians still ask today: if marriage is so significant to God (it is), what happens to that all-important relationship in Heaven?

WHEN THE BEGINNING ENDS
WHAT HAPPENS WHEN WE DIE?

That same day the Sadducees, who say there is no resurrection, came to him with a question. 'Teacher,' they said, 'Moses told us that if a man dies without having children, his brother must marry the widow and raise up offspring for him. Now there were seven brothers among us. The first one married and died, and since he had no children, he left his wife to his brother. The same thing happened to the second and third brother, right on down to the seventh. Finally, the woman died. Now then, at the resurrection, whose wife will she be of the seven, since all of them were married to her?'

Jesus replied, 'You are in error because you do not know the Scriptures or the power of God. At the resurrection people will neither marry nor be given in marriage; they will be like the angels in heaven' (Matthew 22:23-30).

For those who don't have happy marriages or who don't particularly care for their spouse, maybe that's a good thing. But most married people I know are, to put it bluntly, disappointed by this statement of Jesus. We want to believe that something as significant and important as life-long marriage would have a place in Heaven. But let's try to set aside our fallen human emotions for a moment and think dispassionately about what makes marriage a significant institution on earth. Why did God institute it in the Garden?

- God specifically created man to need a helpmate for his work (Genesis 2:18).
- God gifted man to provide a sense of security and protection for his wife (physical, emotional, spiritual).
- God gifted woman to provide a sense of companionship and desire for her husband (physical, emotional, spiritual).
- God gifted both men and women to offer a physical, emotional, and spiritual intimacy for one another.
- God gifted both men and women to be partners in procreation – a necessary act for fulfilling God's command to fill the earth and subdue it (Genesis 1:28).

Those realities are what make the relationship of Godly marriage so significant on earth. And to be blunt, none of them will be needed in Heaven:

- We won't need help for our work.
- We will never feel insecure or unsafe.
- We will never be alone or undesired.
- We will be in a constant state of bliss, overwhelmed by the intimate presence of God.
- We will not need to procreate or reproduce in Heaven.

In other words, the absolute best marriage on earth simply could never compare to the fulfillment of our souls in Heaven. Jesus explains that Himself:

WHEN THE BEGINNING ENDS
WHAT HAPPENS WHEN WE DIE?

And if I go and prepare a place for you, I will come back and take you to be with Me that you also may be where I am (John 14:3).

Forget the spectacular views, the personally fitted accommodations, the familial relationships, and the indescribable beauty of Heaven. All of that is secondary; it is merely the setting for what truly makes Heaven a perfect place. The glory of Heaven was revealed in three words right in the middle of the preceding verse: *be with Me.*

I've been privileged in my life and occupations to do a fair amount of traveling to a number of different places. I've driven to the "casket capital of the world" to speak in a rural church there – the drive through the dark rural woods of an area known for the coffins it produces was not one of my favorite experiences. I've driven to speak at a men's camp that was literally three miles off the nearest road and required me to drive through – yes *through* – a cornfield that had a car path worn down it. I've flown to Colorado to speak at a family conference that was held up on a mountain a mile above the Mile High City itself. I was winded from the altitude only about 5 minutes into my talk.

But without question, the most

aesthetically unrivaled location I've ever been invited to was a place called Marco Island, just off the coast of Florida. The driver that took me from the airport to the resort where I was to speak told me that crime was virtually non-existent on the island. And the surroundings were incredible: waterfalls, infinity pools, beaches that come right up to the pool deck edge, swim-up barstools, perfectly groomed foliage, and soft sand beaches.

It was a wonderful experience, but not nearly as great as it could have been. In fact, the whole time I was there, this was nagging at me and taking away from the trip. I know that makes me sound ungrateful or spoiled, but that's not what I mean. The problem with the trip was that my wife Jenny couldn't go. She had just gotten home with our 3rd child, we had just moved into our new house and there was just no way for her to make the trip with me. And frankly, without her there it wasn't the same. Of course I enjoyed it, but I was always cognizant of the fact that I couldn't enjoy it as much as I would if I had someone I loved there to share it with.

The sunset beaches were wonderful, but what makes them truly special would have been holding Jenny's hand while walking them. The waterfalls through the palm trees and trickling down the rocks was very nice, but

WHEN THE BEGINNING ENDS
WHAT HAPPENS WHEN WE DIE?

what would have been much nicer would have been sitting in front of it having conversation with Jenny. The environment was nice, but it wasn't enough on its own to be perfect. It needed her.

It wasn't that long ago that Jenny and I were sleeping in bed about 2 a.m. when all of a sudden we both were awakened to the sound of our oldest daughter throwing up loudly in her room down the hall. Jenny instinctively threw the covers off to rush in to Addie's side. I instinctively laid there with my eyes shut acting like I hadn't heard a thing and was sound asleep. I knew when Jenny got to the room, because I heard an audible and deliberate, "Oh. My. Gosh." Though I continued feigning sleep, it didn't last long.

Soon Jenny was back in the room shaking me to tell me that she needed help. When I walked through the door I saw why. It looked like a war zone. I was about to start musing how it was even possible for a body that small to have had that much vomit to purge in the first place when I saw her little face around the corner. Poor little thing was almost as mortified by the experience as Jenny and I were. Almost.

We used towels, carpet cleaner, garden hose, washing machine and Lysol in about every corner of that room. At one point during the scrubbing, I looked up at Jenny and started laughing. She had her shirt pulled up over her nose and without cracking a smile she said, "What is so funny?"

I just smirked at her and replied, "It's 2 a.m. My, this is quite a little corner of Heaven we've carved out for ourselves, isn't it?" She started laughing too. And that's the truth – I love our life. I realized in that gross moment that I wouldn't want to clean up barf at 2 a.m. with anyone else in the world.

You take that kind of loving relationship, flawed as it is, and tweak the environment just a tad – like to Marco Island – and it's hard to imagine it getting any better.

But it does. In Heaven, immaculate and breathtaking scenery will be set as the backdrop of an incomparable intimacy we will enjoy with a Savior whose love is anything but flawed. That combination is what makes Heaven a perfect paradise where God's eternal love story unfolds seamlessly complete throughout eternity. Sign me up.

FOURTEEN

THE KING HAS COME

Of course it's true that the excitement and pleasure you get from being with your spouse on Marco Island is directly proportional to the degree to which you like each other. If Jen and I couldn't get along, if I was constantly betraying her, if she was distant and detached, finding ourselves together and alone in a tropical paradise might not be nearly as intimate.

Therefore when Jesus promises us that what will make this land of breathtaking beauty, unending worship, perfected bodies, unimaginable discovery, exceeding familiarity, and incomparable intimacy so amazing is that it will be Him and me, that should be more than a promise. It should be an enticement to cultivate and grow a deeper, increasingly meaningful relationship with Him now. The closer we are now, the better it will be then.

That's precisely how God always wanted it to be.

In essence, what heaven offers is a complete and full reversal of the curse in Eden. Everything that hinders, everything that obstructs, everything that distracts us from our relationship and interaction with God will be removed for eternity – just as it was intended to be from the start.

One of the most fascinating Biblical exercises to do is the very thing that drives literature professors nuts – skip the middle of the book. I remember one of my go-to strategies for writing book reports in school was to read the opening pages of the assigned text to learn character names and personalities. Then I would skip to the end to see who was still alive, where they ended up, how the conflict was resolved. That usually gave me enough to "expand" upon over the course of the mandated 3-5 pages (and a few font and margin adjustments on the formatting could always be used in a pinch).

My teachers would always warn us not to try something like that because we would miss the meat of the story – the tensions, the growth, the love story. And now when I read for fun, I admit that they are completely right about that. But for the purposes of this exercise, I want you to pretend you're me in high school writing a book report over the entire Bible. Go and read the first three chapters of Genesis followed immediately by the last three chapters in Revelation. Yes, you will be skipping the eternal story of God's

WHEN THE BEGINNING ENDS
WHAT HAPPENS WHEN WE DIE?

relentless and amazing redemptive plan for humanity. But I want you to see what I mean by heaven being a reversal of the curse. The first three of Genesis and last three of Revelation offer perfect bookends for the Word.

In the first three chapters of Genesis notice what we lose:

- Heaven on Earth
- Gold and precious gems
- The river running through Eden
- Access to the Tree of Life
- The ability to walk with God
- Perfection without corruption
- Human health and happiness
- Life without death

It's a depressing state of affairs if you stop there. But don't stop – and instead just skip straight to Revelation 20 to see what we regain in Heaven:

- New Heaven and new Earth
- Precious stones and jewels
- The river running through the City
- Access to the Tree of Life
- The ability to dwell with God
- Corruption perfected
- No human sickness or pain
- Life without end

A complete reversal of the curse. It wasn't until I had children that I became a fan of the *Toy Story* movie franchise, but I admit that there are still parts of it I don't like. The movies are incredibly well written, funny, creative, and the technology was certainly cutting edge for their day. My objection is not cinematic; it's sentimental.

As Andy (the boy who owns the toys) gets older, he naturally discards his once beloved playthings to storage containers and orders their banishment to either the attic or the trash can. Watching the emotional trauma those once treasured toys endured haunts me every time I watch. I think about what my poor F-14 Tomcat fighter jet must have felt. I think about my G.I. Joe figures that are probably rotting in an oversized trash sack in some landfill. And my Transformers – my gosh those poor Transformers – that went from being played with every second of the day to being neglected then forgotten.

But that's the story of life on earth. New things don't last. If you want a good reminder of that, go and watch a few of your home movies from Christmas morning. You won't be five minutes into the video before you see something opened that prompts you to say, "Oh man, I had forgotten about that!" Exactly.

And it's not just things. On earth, even new thrills get old. It's why people aren't driving Model T's anymore. It's why theme parks are constantly building bigger, faster roller coasters. It's why some people can't stay content in their marriage. Being conditioned to that kind of environment has a tendency to make us question how an eternal kingdom, no matter how great it may be, would not get old after a few thousand years. John offers us the answer:

> *For the old order of things has passed away. He who was seated on the throne said, "I am making everything new!"* (Revelation 21:4-5)

Understand that means that every second in Heaven will feel like you just arrived. Your eyes will be wide open, everything around you will always be exciting, always new, and you yourself will feel like a brand hew person. Nothing will ever wear down, break down, be forgotten, or grow old. There will never be a hint of boredom or any chance to think about a need for more. More is all there is – a never ending supply of more.

Again, in trying to explain this concept – or even fully understand it myself – I am frustrated by the limits of my physical mind and existence. I know what I'm trying to say, but can find no way to fully encapsulate it or illustrate it through earthly comparisons. All I can do is express what the Father has revealed to us through His Holy Spirit.

James tells us that *Every good and perfect gift is from above, coming down from the Father of the Heavenly Lights, who does not change like shifting shadows* (1:17). This seems to be a fairly simple concept: everything I like on this earth and about this earth comes from God. And everything I don't understand or don't like here on earth is the result of these "shifting shadows." Shadows cross us when we turn away from, or when we are blocked from the source of light.

That's what sin does in our world – it turns us away from, or blocks us from the source of light that is God. In Heaven, there will be no more of these shadows. Nothing will be present to turn us from, or block us from the light of God. Meaning heaven is the embodiment of all the good that we have ever known here. That's why I stress again, if you go to Heaven, this life you are living now is as close to Hell as you will ever be.

Regardless of your earthly circumstances, that truth should change your life into one of immense joy. I heard a preacher once reference the story of Cinderella. Most people know the plot line: a lovely, compassionate, and generous young woman is bossed around by a nasty step-mother and two wicked step-sisters. She is forced to clean and scrub the floors, making her home literally amongst the ashes and "cinders."

All that changes when she attends the Prince's ball, meets him and has a dazzling evening. The night is cut short when the magical spell that brought her to the ball wears off at the stroke of midnight. She scurries away before being transformed back into her rags, and in her haste leaves one of her glass slippers behind. The Prince collects the slipper and begins a kingdom-wide search for his love.

Now, this time don't skip to the end of the story. Observe Cinderella back at her chores, but pay close attention to her face and conduct. There's something different about her. Even as she works in the dirt and ash, she is doing it with a smile. Even her evil siblings can't help but notice her changed demeanor. There's a palpable anticipation that exudes from this impoverished maid as she goes about her drudgery.

It's an anticipation that comes from knowing the Prince is on his way. He is looking for her, and she knows he will not stop until he finds her. She knows that her days of cleaning the stove, emptying the trash, sleeping in the filth, and eating scraps are quickly coming to an end. Hers becomes a life of immense joy regardless of circumstance.

For Christ followers that is our promise. While here on earth we may be locked into depressing conditions, difficult situations, and unfortunate circumstances. We may be victims of cruelty, abuse, or neglect. We may experience a figurative Hell on earth, but in the midst of it all we can continue our work with smiles on our face knowing that the Prince is on his way.[1]

We can know that one day soon the eastern sky is going to split wide open, and amidst the trumpet fanfare from a thousand angels, the Prince will ride up to the gates of our lives on the back of a white horse. And He will reach out His nail-scarred hand and pull us out of our muck and mire and carry us away to His kingdom where we will live with Him forever.

The night is over. The curse is reversed. The King has come.

FIFTEEN

HELL MATTERS

So I guess there's no easy way to tell you this, but the rest of this book is going to be about Hell. Now there's an enticement to keep reading if I've ever written one.

Seriously though, I'm assuming that you picked up this book in the first place because you're intrigued to know and truly desirous to find out what God has revealed to us about the life that occurs after this one we are living. And since God says Hell is a reality of that life for many, you probably knew it was going to be addressed.

But why so many chapters? Why so much time and effort placed on describing it? Why almost double the amount of pages spent discussing the horror of Hell as were spent discussing the greatness of Heaven? I'll give you four reasons why.

First, we live in a state of denial about Hell.

Most every non-Christian rejects its existence, largely believing in annihilation theory as a method of coping with death. "After we die, there is no more, that's just it," they say confidently. And while most Christians don't go for that theory, they still demur at the thought of embracing Hell.

I'm assuming everyone who is reading this book has been to a funeral at some point in your lives. Answer me a serious question: if all you knew was what you heard in that funeral service, have you ever attended one where you weren't left with the impression that the person being buried was enjoying Heaven?

I suppose there are some funerals of rabid atheists you might have attended where the person giving the eulogy is under strict instructions not to mention an afterlife or any hereafter. But for the most part, even at the memorial services for the most non-religious people I've ever known, there is always talk of "seeing that person again someday," or them "looking down on us and smiling," or about them "being in a better place."

And we Christians largely go along with this tendency towards deception, partially because we see no purpose or tact in adding to the suffering or mourning of people by telling them anything that would indicate their dearly departed was anywhere

WHEN THE BEGINNING ENDS
WHAT HAPPENS WHEN WE DIE?

but a happy place.

But I think it is also because while we embrace the truth of Christianity in the church pew, in the funeral home we quickly move towards exchanging it with universalism – the idea that surely God will fix it somehow. Some way, we comfort ourselves, God will bring all people to Him because, after all, God is love and wants no one to perish.

Maybe that's why recent polls have revealed that while 76% of Americans believe in the existence of Heaven, between 6 and 32% believe in the existence of Hell.[1] We are in denial.

Secondly, Jesus spent a great deal of time warning about Hell, so I'm going to also.

A few years ago my wife and I were driving back late at night from Washington, D.C. After promising to help keep me awake by talking to me on our trip back, Jenny had fallen into a deep sleep about 90 seconds into the trip. The interstate was largely deserted that late, but as I rounded one of the curves on I-70 I met a car coming the opposite direction that began to flash his high beams in my face.

My initial reaction was to get agitated and flash him back, assuming he incorrectly thought I was driving with my brights on when I wasn't. But that didn't stop him. For the next 7-10 seconds before we passed each other, he kept doing it. It dawned on me that one of two things had just occurred.

It's possible that he was being kind and letting me know that I was about to drive into either an accident or a speed trap. The other possibility was that it was a gang initiation and I was about to be murdered in Western Pennsylvania while my wife slept peacefully. I hoped for the former, but between you and me I kept checking my rear-view mirror the rest of the night for the latter.

Given that I'm writing this book, it's pretty clear that either it was an extremely incompetent gang, or my initial assumption was right. While I never saw the police officer if he was out there in the dark, I had reduced my speed just a tad as a precaution and tend to believe that the mysterious flasher (be careful how you interpret that) on the interstate that night saved me a traffic stop and a ticket.

When drivers do that for other drivers, they are providing a warning to their fellow man that they are about to encounter the law. At that point you're left with the option of whether you want to heed their warning or blow them off. The reason I chose to heed the driver's warning that late autumn night in Pennsylvania was because I knew he had already been where I was about to go. He knew something I didn't.

When it comes to the afterlife, Jesus has been where we are about to go. And as I read Scripture, I see Him flashing His high beams at us with great frequency and intensity. I find it beyond irresponsible to ignore that and blow Him off.

Third, the job of every Christian according to Scripture is to be Ambassadors of Christ (2 Corinthians 5:20).

As Dr. Evans explains, imagine a doctor looking at your scans, seeing the mass on your lungs and saying to the nurses, "I guess I don't really know what it is, but it's probably nothing. I'm not going to worry about this one or mention it to them."

Or imagine a police officer who saw a group of thugs throwing rocks through your business window, and looting the store in broad daylight, saying to his partner with a chuckle, "Oh geez, boys will be boys, let's just go."

Or how about a fireman who saw the flames climbing the stories of an office building towards trapped workers and said to his fellow fireman, "Honestly that thing will eventually burn itself out – it can't burn forever."[1]

What would you say about those individuals? Amongst other things, we could all unanimously conclude that they do not take their jobs very seriously. In the same way, a Christian who sees what Scripture says about the reality of Hell and does not spend ample time addressing it and warning about it doesn't take his job very seriously either.

And finally, there is not a soul on earth that doesn't need to hear about Hell, for fairly obvious reasons.

For Christians, we need to know what God has saved us from. The more we comprehend the reality of Hell, the more it shatters our ability to underestimate the love God has for us.

For non-Christians, they need to know why they desperately need God to save them.[2] The biggest cure to an apathetic mind ambivalent towards eternal matters is to introduce it to the reality of Hell. If Hell is real, every other concern, every other problem, every other issue pales in comparison to how we deal with it.

So is it real?

SIXTEEN

HOW WE FEEL ABOUT IT

I mentioned briefly in the last chapter the universalist tendency we all want to feel when it comes to the existence of Hell. If there is a God and He *is* love, it seems counterintuitive to even begin to consider that Hell could exist. Francis Chan begins his book Erasing Hell by contrasting two important questions:

> Do you *want* to believe in a God that would send people to Hell
>
> vs.
>
> *Can* you believe in a God that would send people to Hell

Before we come back to those questions, read the words Chan speaks in his video introduction to the book:

"The other day the image came to my mind of Romans 9 where God compares me to a piece of clay. And He says 'You're like a piece of clay and I'm the potter.' And so just that I thought, 'Wow, that means I'm like a piece of clay trying to explain to other pieces of clay what the Potter is like.'

Think about that for a second. It shows the silliness for any of us to think we're an expert on Him. Our only hope is that He would reveal to us what He is like and then we can just repeat those things.

In Psalm 25 verse 9, He talks about how He explains His way to those who are humble. And so I'm like, 'Okay God I wanna be humble then because I gotta know the truth about you. Humble me. Show me the pride in my life.'

See and that's why I've been concerned as I've listened to some of the discussion about Hell and read some of these things that are written…Maybe the thing I'm most concerned about is this arrogance.

Look, in Isaiah 55 God says, 'Your thoughts are not like my thoughts. And your ways are not as my ways.' He goes, 'As high as the heavens are above the earth, that's how much higher my ways are than your ways. That's how much higher my thoughts are than your thoughts.'

So when we begin an argument with, 'Well, I wouldn't believe in a God who would –' Who would what? Do something that you wouldn't do? Or think in a way that's different from the way you think? Do you ever even consider the possibility that maybe the Creator's sense of justice is actually more developed than yours? And maybe His love and His mercy are perfect, and that you could be the one that is flawed?

See when we make statements like, 'Well God wouldn't do this, would He?' do you understand at that moment you're actually putting God's actions in submission to your reasoning? You're in essence saying, 'Well God wouldn't think that way or act that way because I wouldn't act that way or think that way.'"[1]

That's a powerful indictment of all of us. We all do that. There are things that you and I as humans urgently want to believe are true or not true, and we often times approach our debates about religious or moral issues with the preconceived notion of what we believe God *ought* to think or do. That vain attitude actually attempts to put God's conduct under the judgment of our mortal sense of morality.

That is what I have tried so desperately to avoid in this book, and am desperately seeking to avoid in these next several chapters. I want to approach the topic of Hell with great humility, speak where God speaks and be silent where God is silent.

With that said, let's return to Chan's original two questions. Enlightened man's thinking today is that Hell isn't a rational thought. In our state of evolved cultural morality we just can't fathom a God who would send people to eternal torment. And so the answer to the first question of whether we *want* to believe in a God who punishes non-Christians forever is fairly simple.

No. No, we don't.

Now, don't get pious on me. Don't remove yourself from the personal side of this. Think about your non-Christian friends. So many of them are kind and pleasant and genial and warm and gracious. Do you *want* a God that makes them spend eternity in Hell?

I'll answer that. Here's what I want given my sense of justice: I want these non-Christian offenders to spend time in punishment equal to their offenses. If they are merely average sinners who have offended God with lies and gossip, their punishment should be shorter than those who have offended God with murders and rapes. After their time has been spent and they have submitted to Christ and exhibited true repentance and acceptance, let them into Heaven.

That's what my fallen sense of justice thinks seems fair. (Notice I said fallen – I think it's important to remember what Chan was getting at earlier that it might just be possible that my Creator's sense of justice and understanding of fairness might just be a bit more developed and more perfect than my own.)

Sometimes when talking with skeptics I will ask them this question. I will ask if they could have been God if they would send people to everlasting punishment. Many say, "No that's horrible." What's interesting about that response is that it is appealing to a moral authority. Where, in other words, did they get their sense of fairness and justice that tells them eternal punishment is "horrible?"

Appealing to an absolute morality demands an absolute moral law, which demands an absolute, authoritative moral Lawgiver – the very thing they are skeptical about in the first place.

It's usually at that point in time that I introduce them to the story of Bill Benefiel. Bill was a man who lived in my then-home town of Terre Haute, Indiana in the mid-1980s. He was the reason my parents were very cautious of allowing my brother and I to play outside alone or go on bike rides too far from our small neighborhood.

According to the serial killer crime index:

> The State's case was established by a surviving victim, 17-year-old Alicia, who was kidnapped on the way to a store in Terre Haute by Benefiel, armed with a gun and wearing a mask.
>
> Alicia was tied-up and gagged, driven to Benefiel's home and taken inside. During 4 months of captivity inside Benefiel's home, Alicia was raped and sodomized over 60 times at gunpoint. Most of this time she was chained and handcuffed to a bed. He glued her eyelids shut, put tape over her eyes, and toilet paper in her mouth. She was cut with a knife and beaten.
>
> After 3 months, Alicia saw a second girl, Delores Wells, in the home. She was naked and handcuffed on the bed, with tape over her eyes and mouth. She later saw Benefiel beat Delores and put superglue in her nose, then pinch it together.
>
> Benefiel left the home for 2 hours and

upon his return, confessed to Alicia that he had killed and buried Delores.

When police knocked on the door, Benefiel stuffed Alicia into a ceiling crawl space. The police entered with a search warrant and rescued her. The body of Delores was found soon after in a wooded area. An autopsy established asphyxia as the cause of death.[2]

Whenever I tell this story to the skeptic, they are horrified and quickly acknowledge that if they were God, some form of serious (perhaps even torturous) punishment seems appropriate, but eternity seems too long. In other words, they become fickle and inconsistent, unsure about the duration appropriate and even conflicted about the kind of punishment that's suitable. Proximity to or relation with the victim of a crime also messes with our fragile human sense of justice.

Again, back to Chan: is it possible the Creator's sense of justice is more developed than our own? That hardly seems even remotely difficult to answer. Of course it's possible. It must be.

And if that's the case, even though it seems obvious to us that we don't want to believe in a God that punishes people eternally, we have to move on to the more important question: can we believe in such a God?

SEVENTEEN

WHAT GOD SAYS ABOUT IT

I suppose there's no delicate way to put this, so I won't try. Instead I will just say candidly that what you and I want to believe about God is completely and utterly irrelevant.

I mean, I guess it would matter if we were sitting around a coffee table at Starbucks, having deep, philosophical exchanges about how we would rule the universe. But with all due respect, that conversation will never happen between us because I'm totally uninterested in how you would exercise supreme cosmic power. And for the record, I would expect you to be totally uninterested in how I would do so.

After all, unless we're the most egotistical narcissists in the world, we'd have to admit that if given that power, we'd both screw it up pretty badly.

Along those lines, I'm truly incapable of describing how little I care about the god or gods that you or anyone else wants to believe in. Your sense of justice is inherently flawed, your perspective remarkably narrow, your understanding imperfect, your wisdom inadequate, and your experiences absurdly limited. Mine too.

That's why from the very beginning of this book I've made clear that I'm only interested (and I'm assuming you're still reading because you're only interested) in what the Bible says about the God who actually does exist. This entire text has been about letting God speak for Himself. God instructs, and He doesn't ask for our input; He asks for us to listen and learn. The wise among us will do just that.

As Dr. Evans writes,

> "Your reason about this subject (of Hell) must be made subject to God's revelation. How you feel about it must be subjected to what God says about it."[1]

That's exactly right. So what does He say? In Matthew 25, Jesus gives us an important glimpse of judgment, saying,

> *Then He will say to those on His left, 'Depart from Me, you who are cursed, into the eternal fire prepared for the Devil and his angels'...then they will go away to*

eternal punishment, but the righteous to eternal life. (Matthew 25: 41, 46)

For the increasingly large number of Christians who profess that there is no Hell, and for the even larger number of Christians who regardless of what they say, behave like there is no Hell (see the funeral home), this is a blunt contradiction coming from the Savior we claim to follow. There is no ambiguity in these words of Christ.

Reading them, we must conclude that if in fact Hell is *not* real, then Scripture isn't trustworthy and Jesus Himself is a liar. Why would any Christian call themselves such if they believe those things? If they believe that Jesus is a liar about something as significant as the eternal fate of mankind, why would they ever turn to Him or trust Him on topics He spent far less time discussing and explaining? Remember that Christ's warnings about Hell are not confined to this mere passage. Those red letters in your Bible reveal Jesus spending far more time talking about Hell than He did Heaven or love. So why would we trust His promise of Heaven, or listen to His counsel on love, if we reject, disregard, ignore, or explain away His plain teaching on the eternal reality of Hell?

There's one answer to that question: our feelings. We don't *want* to believe in Hell, so we choose to ignore what is plainly described for us in this passage.

In Matthew 25, Jesus explicitly affirms that there

is a place of eternal exile where the ungodly experience God's retribution against sin. And that word retribution is an important one for us to commit to memory. This should be our choice of vocabulary when discussing Hell, even more than we use the term punishment.

I'm sure Jenny and I are not the only parents guilty of executing a punishment against our children that has been disproportionate to the offense they committed. Like all parents, we can get so frustrated with our children that we get carried away:

> Me: You broke her toy after I told you not to mess with it? That's it, you go to your room for the rest of the day with no toys.
>
> Grayson: But daddy, I...
>
> Me: Don't talk, just go to your room. For the rest of the day I don't want to see you out of there!
>
> Jenny: (whispers) Hey, Stalin, you do realize it's 8:30 in the morning, right?

Punishments are sometimes unjust because they reflect our emotions more than they reflect our judgment. That's why a lot of parents opt to send their children into exile for a few moments as they gather their thoughts and decide on the appropriate penalty to fit the crime. For the record, that's what my parents often did, and I absolutely hated those moments, sitting in silence, waiting to hear Dad's footsteps coming down the hall to lay out my sentence.

Now, while God certainly doesn't need any cooling-off period to know what is appropriate punishment, I think the word retribution is the best to use for the sake of our own understanding. It prevents us from getting the wrong idea about what is happening in Hell. It's not the result of God's temper-tantrum. It is perfect justice for crimes committed.

Christian theology soundly explains the purpose and cause of death on earth. It is the *temporary* reality of the presence of sin (Romans 5:12, 1 Corinthians 15:21). The second death known as Hell, is the *eternal* reality of the same. And notice that word eternal.

In the original Greek language, the word *aiônios* is used to describe the duration of Hell. That's very instructive given the fact that it is the same word chosen to describe the duration of Heaven and the duration of God Himself. Christians who reject the eternality of Hell foolishly and inadvertently call into question some extremely foundational principles of the faith. If Hell is not forever, Heaven isn't, and God may not be either.

WHEN THE BEGINNING ENDS
WHAT HAPPENS WHEN WE DIE?

In questioning the eternality of Hell we also must ignore what would be the inexplicably extreme warning Jesus gives in Matthew 18:

> *If your hand or your foot causes you to stumble, cut it off and throw it away. It is better for you to enter life maimed or crippled than to have two hands or two feet and be thrown into eternal fire. And if your eye causes you to stumble, gouge it out and throw it away. It is better for you to enter life with one eye than to have two eyes and be thrown into the fire of Hell.* (Matthew 18: 8-9)

If Hell is temporary or short-lived, this instruction is absurdly and irresponsibly harsh, is it not? Jesus is saying:

- If there's somewhere you choose to go (your foot causing you to stumble)
- If there's something you choose to look at (your eye causing you to stumble)

It is better to maim yourself by chopping them off for the duration of your earthly life than to let them take you down a path towards Hell. Jesus is serious about Hell because it is terrible and it is eternal.

If I'm His follower, I trust that His teachings and warnings are true. Which seems to beg the question...

EIGHTEEN

WHY HELL?

Why Hell? Why create it? Why subject us to the possibility of it if He truly loves us?

I recently got this email from a reader that reflects many of the same questions I have had and perhaps you have had about Hell:

> "I have a couple of questions that I was hoping you might shed some light on. My mortal and created brain thinks that eternity in hell is too harsh for the unbeliever. [It] makes me think that free will is NOT a blessing, but a curse. I don't want free will. Why would God create human beings only to suffer in hell for eternity? Would it not be better for humans if we were not created at all in the first place? Why would God set up

such a system?"

I'd venture to say that the inability to come to a satisfactory answer to some of those very questions is what has driven some people into either disbelief in the God of Christianity, or disbelief in Hell. It prompts us, driven by emotion, to conclude either Hell doesn't exist, or I cannot worship a God who would create such a place.

Let me reiterate that coming to faith in Christ means being convinced that He is the Son of God. It means accepting the truth of His revelation. It means believing and knowing that His ways are far above our ways, and His thoughts are incomprehensible for our meager minds.

Meaning, if we truly believe, then there must be an element of childlike faith that says, "Even if I can't get satisfactory answers to the questions that burn within me, I'm confident those answers do exist, and I trust God regardless of my inability to understand." It exudes confidence even in the absence of clear answers.

There's only one example I can think of that reflects it: the way my son Grayson trusts me if I tell him something.

> Grayson: I'm too high. You can't reach me up here on the diving board.

Me: No you're not. I'll be right there under you.

Grayson: If I jump in, I will sink.

Me: No you won't. I'll keep your head above water.

Grayson: You can't catch me; you'll sink too.

Me: No, I won't. I'll catch you.

Grayson: It will hurt if I jump from here.

Me: No, it won't. I won't let it.

Grayson: I won't be able to breathe if I'm in the water.

Me: You won't have to. I'll hold you up.

Grayson: Okay. *closes eyes and jumps*

That's exactly the kind of humble faith I believe Jesus told us to exhibit:

> He called a little child to him, and placed the child among them. And he said: "Truly I tell you, unless you change and become like little children, you will never enter the kingdom of heaven. Therefore, whoever takes the lowly position of this child is the greatest in the kingdom of heaven

(Matthew 18:2-4).

Please understand, having childlike faith doesn't mean having a childish faith. There's an important distinction between the two. Little children can be led astray by fantasies and myths, while Christians are exhorted to become mature in our thinking:

> *Brothers and sisters, stop thinking like children. In regard to evil be infants, but in your thinking be adults* (1 Corinthians 14:20).

> *He is the one we proclaim, admonishing and teaching everyone with all wisdom, so that we may present everyone fully mature in Christ* (Colossians 1:28).

My children do not jump off the diving board into the arms of just any adult. They wouldn't even get near a pool with an adult they didn't know or trust. But since they know me, know I love them, and have seen credible evidence of my reliability in other areas of their lives, they are willing to trust me on the things they don't fully understand. They are developing a mature confidence in my love and concern for them and it affects their willingness to trust my faithfulness in areas beyond their comprehension or logic.

Even if we could never comprehend the appropriateness or perfection of God's justice, we must have developed a mature confidence in His complete love and righteousness. We know His place and our place, and therefore put trust in His faithfulness in those areas that are beyond our logical grasp.

That said, I do believe God gives us some important answers to the question, "Why Hell?" that we too often overlook or ignore. Let me start with a hypothetical.

I live in a nice, quiet neighborhood in Kokomo, Indiana. There aren't a lot of children in our neighborhood but suppose there were. And suppose that in my backyard I constructed a large fire pit. And suppose that one day you see me on the street and someone says to you, "Do you know that guy burns children alive in his fire pit?" Shocked, you do more research and find out that it's true. You discover that a great number of neighborhood children have been burned alive in my fire pit.

What would you think of me? Maniac? Cruel? Monster?

But then suppose you found out that things aren't exactly as they seem. Suppose you found out that my neighborhood had a terrible problem with venomous snakes (something Kokomo, Indiana is obviously well known for). And as it turned out, I had constructed my fire pit for the sole purpose of burning all the dangerous snakes that were after the children. I worked tirelessly, giving of myself, my time, my resources, my energies, everything I was, to catch those snakes and burn them before they hurt anyone. You saw the scars on my arms from the snakebites I had endured. You saw the burn marks from the times I got a little too close to the fire trying to dispose of them.

Your perspective on me might begin to change. But still – I may be burning snakes, but that doesn't excuse me burning children too.

And then you find out that I've never burned a child myself. Instead, for some reason, the kids in the neighborhood were obsessed with these snakes. They were fascinated by them – which is one reason I knew I had to round them all up and destroy them as fully as possible. And as it happened, when I was working to round up snakes, some children inexplicably dove into the fire themselves, chasing snakes. When I found out they were doing that, I was heartbroken. I put up a massive fence, I put up warning signs, I reached out to parents in the neighborhood to train their children to stay away, and I even hired workers to go around canvasing the neighborhood teaching the kids to stay away from the fire.

Yet still, despite all our work of warning them, some of the children continued to slip through and jump into the fire. I considered just removing the fire pit, but I know that if I do that, the snakes will overrun the neighborhood and kill everyone. So I press on doing all I can to burn the snakes and keep everyone else away from the fire.

How do you view me now? Still a monster? Or maybe something completely different?

I know that's a weak and somewhat silly analogy, but the truth is that our startling lack of understanding as to why Hell exists causes our perception of God to be horribly skewed. Look at what Jesus teaches:

> *Then he will say to those on his left, 'Depart from me, you who are cursed, into the eternal fire prepared for the devil and his angels'* (Matthew 25:41).

Did you catch the last seven words of that sentence? Hell was never designed for us. The fire pit was designed for the snakes. That's all God wants to burn. Yet inexplicably, against His best efforts and to His great dismay, the precious children He wants so desperately to save insist on jumping into the fire with the snakes either because they have been deceived about the fire or simply don't take its danger seriously.

Both Ezekiel 28 and Isaiah 14 are helpful chapters in understanding "why Hell." In vivid language, even if sparing details, God explains that Satan and his angels chose to live apart from God. Prideful and arrogant, Satan desired the throne of God Himself, and

WHEN THE BEGINNING ENDS
WHAT HAPPENS WHEN WE DIE?

ignorantly rebelled against Him. I often tell my students in American history class when we get to the country's revolution against Britain that it's a general rule of thumb historically speaking that if you're going to rebel against the master, you'd better win. If you don't, you haven't signed a Declaration of Independence, you've signed your death warrant.

In Satan's rebellion against God, he did exactly that. The creature unsurprisingly lost his revolt against the Creator, and God crafted Hell as an eternal reminder of the consequences of spiritual rebellion. The duration of Hell then becomes self-explanatory – it is eternal because its subjects (Satan and his angels) are eternal.

Hell was never designed with human beings in mind. It was created solely as the destination of all those who chose it. Satan chose to go to Hell – he picked it over living an existence that was submissive or second to God. He wanted a world removed from the presence of God, and he received it. Hell wasn't the consequence of chance for Satan; it was the consequence of choice.

And the human beings who are there have found themselves in that place only because they made the same choice. That probably seems confusing because it implies that people willfully, openly, and intentionally proclaim their desire to go into eternal punishment. It conjures up silly mental images of a person standing before the judgment seat of God, looking at his two options and asking for eternal damnation where there is weeping and gnashing of teeth.

No one actually says, "I'd like to be in Hell, thank you." But people do say every day, "I don't want Jesus, thank you." And if there are only two paths, as Christian theology certainly teaches (Matthew 7:13-14; Proverbs 14:12), rejecting one path is necessarily choosing the other.

> (Let me briefly pause to acknowledge the extenuating circumstances related to infants and toddlers, the insane, and those whose remote location on earth leaves them in a position where they have never heard the Gospel of Jesus nor been presented with the choice of these two explicit paths. Exceptional resources and books exist that dive into these issues. This is not one of those books for one primary reason: none of those circumstances apply to anyone who is reading this book.)

Yet there's still something that doesn't add up. Why did God continue with the plan when He saw His precious creations choosing Hell? Go back to the analogy of my fire pit and the question seems obvious: "Once you see those kids jumping into the pit, why didn't you put out the fire? Why did you not shut it down and go to Plan B?"

I'm not disregarding the question, but it is

nevertheless important to highlight that by asking that, we are again back to concocting the kind of god we think we want to worship. We are again back to judging the morality of our Creator, assuming that my moral code is better developed than His – even though He gave me my moral code to begin with. We are again back to saying that this God thing doesn't add up simply because He did something that we wouldn't have done.

Maybe it would be helpful to get a better handle on this by thumbing through the pages of Scripture and noticing just how frequently God does things that you and I wouldn't have done. Francis Chan challenges us to do that, and I think it's a good exercise in humility and self-awareness for us.

Would you have chosen to wipe out all humanity for their sinful depravity, and included the vast majority of wildlife in the carnage? Would you have chosen to conduct this annihilation through the waters of a great flood? Would you have chosen to spare the few that survived by making them build a boat over the course of 100 years, detailed to extraordinary specifications?

Would you have punished a man named Achan for looting some property that wasn't his after a battle against a vile enemy? Would you have carried out a death sentence against him even after his seeming sincere confession and apology? Would you have conducted his execution by having him stoned?

Would you have then seen to it that his family was stoned? To finish it off, would you have had the bodies and possessions of Achan and his family burned to nothing?

Would you have required your prophet Ezekiel to lay on his right side for 390 days, followed by having him lay on his left side for 40 days? Would you have ordered him to cook food over human feces? Would you have instructed him to preach R-rated sermons to the people?

Would you have chosen to save the very people who would still hate you before, during, and after you've done so? Would you have chosen, if having all options at your disposal, to enter the world through lowliness and poverty? Would you allow your own Son to be tortured on behalf of those who mock him and despise him?

I wouldn't have done any of that. And we could keep going and going, finding on almost every page of Scripture another action God takes that I might not have taken myself. Yet contemplating those questions ask me to do something absurd. They ask me to take on the identity of a God I can't even comprehend.

I can't pretend that my responses would be more compassionate or just because I can't even begin to approach an eternal understanding of justice or compassion. I don't know all things; I can't see all things; I can't understand the heart of all men; I can't know the future before it happens.

God's ways are unthinkable and inexplicable. Just try to wrap your mind around this complex truth: God doesn't just act in a compassionate or just way, God *is* compassion. He *is* justice. In other words, when we begin trying to measure someone's compassion or justice, we have to do that against some standard or measuring stick. That standard and measuring stick *is* God. Meaning whatever He does must be good and right. God doesn't just get the right answers, He is the answer key.

Recognizing that should provoke us to repent of our unmitigated arrogance in demanding that God justify Himself to us, and then it should motivate us into prostrating humility. As Chan writes,

> "Scripture is filled with divine actions that don't fit our human standards of logic or morality. But they don't need to because we are the clay and He is the Potter. We need to stop trying to domesticate God or confine Him to tiny categories and compartments that reflect our human sentiments rather than His inexplicable ways."[1]

Amen. In other words, why Hell? Because God deemed it right and just, that's why.

NINETEEN

HOW YOU GET THERE

Every year it happens in my classroom. A student will miss the day of a test for an orthodontist appointment or an illness. Then when they return to school and report to my class, I tell them I need them to go make up their test. Here's how the conversation almost always unfolds:

> Me: You need to go make up the test you missed yesterday.
>
> Them: Now?
>
> Me: Well, why not?
>
> Them: I'm not ready for it today.
>
> Me: But it was yesterday.
>
> Them: I know, but I wasn't here yesterday.

WHEN THE BEGINNING ENDS
WHAT HAPPENS WHEN WE DIE?

Me: Right, but you were to be ready for it yesterday like everybody else. Therefore if you were, you would be ready for it today.

Them: Mr. Heck, seriously, I need to do good on this test.

Me: I know.

Them: Can I please study tonight and take it tomorrow?

Me: (Because I'm a giant pushover) Okay, but don't forget.

They always forget. Sometimes for weeks. Sometimes even longer. And when they never make it up, and the nine weeks grading period ends, that blank grade in the computer automatically rolls over into a 0%, crushing their class average. And that means another conversation ensues:

Them: Um, I just looked at my grade and it says I have an F.

Me: I see. Well, that probably means you failed.

Them: Yeah, but it's all because of this one 0 on that test.

Me: Yes, a 0 on a test would

certainly pull your grade down.

Them: But don't you remember, that was the one you guys took when I was gone.

Me: I honestly don't remember the day we took that, but I believe you that you were gone that day. Why didn't you make it up?

Them: I didn't know about it or I forgot.

Me: I'm guessing you forgot. So what exactly do you want me to do?

Them: Can you let me take it now and even though I know I will fail it, it will at least be a higher percentage F so it doesn't kill my overall grade?

Now, I don't have to tell you what happens these days if a teacher says no to that request. Parents get involved, principals get involved, sometimes federal marshals and the United Nations Security Council gets involved.

With as frustrating as that nearly annual exchange has become, it is a perfect illustration of the absurdity of humanity. When we are denied free will or our choices, we scream about the deprivation of our rights. But when we are granted our choices and free will, we scream about the consequences and demand someone remove them from us.

In the school scenario, my student wanted the choice to make up the test later. I granted it to him. But when given his free will, he made a bad decision to not make it up in time, suffered the consequence for it, and then wanted me to remove the negative outcome for what his own choice brought upon him.

In the case of humanity and our relationship to God, we demand our free will. We don't want to be puppets that do whatever God programs us to do. We want to make our own choices, have our own minds, and be free moral agents with the capacity to choose the direction of our lives. But then when we — or someone else — use free will to make bad choices, we shake our fist at God and demand He fix it since, after all, He has the power to and says He loves us.

God gives us free moral agency to make our own choices. But when one of us drives drunk and kills an innocent family, we then start questioning how a just and good God could have ever allowed such a bad thing to happen. That's intellectual inconsistency of the highest order. We are emotional beings that really struggle to think sometimes.

The same is true about the choice to choose Hell.

According to Scripture, man was designed above all other creatures in God's universe. Bearing the image of his Creator, man is an eternal being set above soulless animals, plants, inanimate objects, and even the angels. The famous evangelist of the Great Awakening, Jonathan Edwards, explained why man will always exceed even the angels:

1. Angels were made to serve God by serving man, but man was made to serve God directly.
2. Human grace, holiness, and love are greater virtues than angelic wisdom and strength.
3. Believers are united to Christ in a way that angels never will be.[1]

It's a fascinating study, but this much we know for certain: man *alone* bears the image of God. That gives him a unique eternal significance. And because he is eternally significant, it is only logical that the choices he makes will be eternally significant. But if there was no Hell, no place of eternal torment for those who choose it, then man and his choices would be uncritical, insignificant, and eternally meaningless. That is not how God created us.

We are given the free will to choose our eternal destiny. It is beyond foolish to demand that freedom, but then complain about its consequences.

For several years my Dad was a prosecuting attorney, but for a short time also maintained a side practice where he would create wills, handle estates, and facilitate legal agreements and contracts. Two things he abjectly refused to participate in were divorces and custody battles. Obviously those are realities in our world and I'm not suggesting that Dad did so out of some sense that he was making a higher moral choice than attorneys who offer those services. I tend to believe Dad couldn't do it because it would have broken his heart.

I've seen one custody battle take place up close and personal in the lives of some friends of mine. And after watching it, I knew exactly why as an attorney I would have no part in it. It's excruciating, particularly when the children are very young.

In most states, when a child reaches the age of accountability, they are allowed to choose who they want to live with – mom or dad. Barring some extenuating circumstance that the child doesn't fully comprehend, the courts allow them to make that life-altering decision. That was the case in the custody battle I witnessed, and I don't know that I will ever get over the devastation I saw in the parent who wasn't chosen.

But here's why that matters to our discussion of Hell. Satan chose rebellion to God, and in a manner of speaking, he moved out of the Father's house and will be living apart from Him forever. What remains to be settled is the custody battle that is currently raging between Satan and God over humanity. Both of them desperately want us to live with them. All of us who have reached the age of accountability get to make our choice. And in this case, it's one or the other — there won't be visitation in eternity.²

In understanding this issue (as best we can, given that we lack the mind and full capacity of God), it can't be repeated too often: neutral, unaligned, dispassionate, average people do not go to Hell. Sinners go to Hell. Meaning that those who choose to sin are picking where they want to go and who they want to live with. And I can only imagine that the pain I saw in the un-chosen parent during my friends' custody battle is magnified a million times over when experienced by our Heavenly Father as we reject Him. And we all have. Romans tell us plainly:

> *There is no one righteous, not even one; there is no one who understands; there is no one who seeks God. All have turned away, they have together become worthless; there is no one who does good, not even one* (Romans 3:10-12).

And again a few verses later, *For all have sinned and fall short of the glory of God* (Romans 3:23). What this means is that each and every one of us have made our choice. And therefore, if every single one of us went to Hell it would be just. Our choices brought us to the gates of Hell and we have no one to blame for that reality but ourselves. To be forced to face the consequences isn't malevolence on God's part; it's justice.

WHEN THE BEGINNING ENDS
WHAT HAPPENS WHEN WE DIE?

If you're still struggling to accept that, make this issue personal. Think back to the last time you witnessed a true injustice:

- An elderly person losing their life savings because they trusted a phone scammer who will never be caught
- A murderer walking free because of a technicality during the collection of evidence
- A pervert admits to sexual assault but the statute of limitations has expired and he can't be tried

Whenever we see these things, it gnaws at us. It isn't fair, we know it, and we long for a way to make it right – some of us even consider vigilante justice in the hope that it might at least bring some peace or closure to the victims.

Until we had officially exhausted every single episode ever made of the program, my wife and I were obsessed with a television series called "Forensic Files." First, it had the greatest narrator voice of all time in Peter Thomas. Second, it was fascinating to see how a random fiber found on a piece of shag carpet could end up bringing the bad guy to justice. And finally, we appreciated the show because it always left you with a satisfying sense of resolution – the bad guys got what was coming to them. We long for that feeling as human beings.

It's why people remain fascinated and even uneasy with unsolved murders like that of 6-year-old Jon

Benet Ramsey. In fact, not to overstate the case, but our insatiable need for justice as humans is precisely why we have judicial systems in every civilized corner of the world. Have you ever paused to consider why that urge is so strong? Animals do not have such systems of retribution – so why us? The answer is self-evident: because we are made in the image of God and thus attributes of His perfect character are reflected in our imperfect character.

Writing as the Apostle to the non-Jewish Gentiles, Paul explains God's inherent sense of justice by saying, *Behold therefore the goodness and severity of God: on them which fell, severity; but towards you, goodness* (Romans 11:22). That stands as an excellent depiction of the full character of God – complete goodness and complete justice.

And that's why we must take the reality of Hell extremely seriously, because the underlying principle regarding its existence is the very character of God. The prophets tell us His *eyes are too pure to look on evil* (Habakkuk 1:13). He can't even **look** at evil. Not only that but, *the Lord will not leave the guilty unpunished* (Nahum 1:3). And our own experience tells us the same. If we can't overlook injustice, if it keeps us up at night, stirs us to anger, if we must respond to it, how much more for our God whose sense of justice is so much keener than our own?

So often when we read passages like that one in Nahum, where a verse earlier the text tells us God *takes vengeance on his foes*, and *is filled with wrath* (Nahum 1:2), we get the wrong idea. When Paul writes that *the wrath of God is being revealed from heaven* (Romans 1:18), we mistake what we're seeing as arbitrary or capricious destruction on God's part. Look at the rest of that verse from Paul about **why** God's wrath is being revealed:

> *The wrath of God is being revealed from Heaven against all the Godlessness and wickedness of people who suppress the truth by their wickedness.* (Romans 1:18)

This isn't violence or hatred. It is righteous retribution against sin, and it manifests in two ways according to Scripture. First, we experience it in God lifting His protective hand. He allows, because of our own persistent choices, Satan and sin to do what they will without His grace or protection acting as a buffer or shield. That is what is meant in the first chapter of Romans where *God gave them over in the sinful desires of their hearts...God gave them over to shameful lusts... God gave them over to a depraved mind* (Romans 1:24, 26, 28). This is the reality of God looking at the unrepentant sinner and saying, "Your will be done."

Secondly there is the active wrath of God where He personally executes the punishment Himself. In the Old Testament, that took the form of Sodom and Gomorrah being destroyed by burning sulfur from Heaven, or the world being extinguished in the waters of Noah's Great Flood. It is also what we are promised is coming for those who doggedly remain in unrepentant sin:

> *But because of your stubbornness and your unrepentant heart, you are storing up wrath against yourself for the day of God's wrath, when His righteous judgment will be revealed.* (Romans 2:5)

Whenever I talk about this with people, it is amazing how many times some will ask, "Are you trying to scare me?" My response is always the same: "Scare *you?* I don't have time for that because I'm terrifying myself!" Of course it's scary! We're talking about the God of the Universe here, who spoke things into existence with just His words, who controls everything from the orbits of planets and the spinning of galaxies to the number of eyelashes on every human face. He is omnipotent, omniscient, omnipresent, and knows my sinful inner thoughts better than I do. There's a reason that the writer of Hebrews cautions, *it is a dreadful thing to fall into the hands of the living God* (Hebrews 10:31). How could we **not** *fear the one who is able to destroy both body and soul in Hell* (Matthew 10:28)?

But let me be clear: I don't fear God throwing a temper-tantrum. That isn't His character. I fear God's righteous attitude toward sin in light of the fact that I am a sinner; and if Paul claimed to be *the worst* (1 Timothy 1:15) of sinners, then I must be the worst of the worst. I can't take such truth lightly – not when the entire testimony of Scripture is telling me not to.

I think that's what shocks me the most about those who claim to be Christ followers, but who reject the idea of Hell. This universalist teaching was most recently voiced within Christendom by celebrity author and former preacher Rob Bell. He wrote in "Love Wins," his scandalous work that marked his divorce from Christianity:

> "Given enough time, everybody will turn to God and find themselves in the joy and peace of God's presence. The love of God will melt every hard heart, and even the most 'depraved sinners' will eventually give up their resistance and turn to God."[3]

As I mentioned, this was the point at which Bell chose to walk away from orthodox Christianity – something later startlingly defined by the *New Yorker* as Bell's search for a "more forgiving faith."[4] But don't make the mistake of thinking that is why Bell's ministry is over. There are plenty of people desperate for answers, and in an era where New Age spiritualism can be conveniently packaged in Christian language and peddled to the masses – particularly on the campuses of America's supposedly Christian universities, there was still a massive market for Bell's kind of preaching.

No, the reason his ministry collapsed is because

there was no longer any need for it. Stop and think about it. By coming to this conclusion about Hell and the lack of eternal retribution for unrepentant sinfulness, and then publicizing it, Bell left his parishioners with two possibilities:

1. If he's wrong and there is a Hell, he is a dangerous false prophet that is endangering their souls and the souls of their children. So it's time to get out.
2. If he's right and there is no Hell, instead there is just an inevitable death that comes regardless of what we do, why not live as though there are no consequences to our actions? Why stay and discipline ourselves to a moral restraint that doesn't ultimately matter?

With either option, any rational congregant at Bell's church would have been forced to conclude, "We're better off without you." An interesting approach to ministry, to be sure.

For me, I just don't feel important or smart enough to concoct my own theories on the afterlife, or to try to outthink the plain words of the prophets, reinterpret the plain words of Jesus, and bastardize the plain words of Paul. I am not qualified to stand on my own authority to proclaim anything to you about a place I've never seen. All I am willing to do is to stand on the authority of the Word alone when I tell you that Hell is real, and what punches our ticket isn't God's capriciousness or unpredictability. It's done at our own request.

TWENTY

GLIMPSES OF HELL

For the last several chapters I've been spending time establishing the reality of Hell. But what about the *realities* of Hell? What is it like, what do those who go truly experience, what do we actually know about it?

Several well-known scholars and theologians have weighed in, with some of the more famous ones claiming to have actually been given glimpses of this everlasting abyss. St. Teresa of Avila, Sister Lucy of Fatima, Bill Wiese and others have all popularized their claims, testifying respectively:

> "The ground seemed to be saturated with water, mere mud. I felt a fire in my soul. I cannot see how it is possible to describe it. My bodily sufferings were unendurable. I saw that there would be

no intermission, nor any end to them."[1]

"We saw a vast sea of fire. Plunged in this fire we saw the demons and the souls of the damned."[2]

"No mercy existed in that place. I was horrified as I heard the screams of an untold multitude of people crying out in torment. It was absolutely deafening."[3]

All of those descriptions seem to fit, in some degree, the picture painted in Scripture, but I obviously can't affirm the accuracy or veracity of any of their claims. What I can do is tell you how the Bible describes it.

In my research, I asked a lot of experts and theologians the question, "What is Hell like?" One of the most fascinating and poignant answers that I received came from a minister who told me, "Quit looking in Revelation and flip back to the other end of the book." I was blown away at the fact that Genesis 1 may offer the most accurate depiction of Hell this side of eternity.

Now the earth was formless and empty, darkness was over the surface of the deep (Genesis 1:2).

From the very beginning of the Bible we know that God had already banished Satan from his heavenly position to the Earth that had been created below. Apart from God's creative presence, Genesis tells us that Earth was a void, dark, swamp. If Hell is a domain completely isolated from God's creative presence, we have no reason to believe it won't be the same: a barren wasteland (sometimes referred to in Scripture as Hades) separated from God's goodness.

We also know that no one ever leaves Hell. And here's why:

> *And the devil, who deceived them, was thrown into the lake of burning sulfur, where the Beast and the False Prophet had been thrown. They will be tormented day and night for ever and ever...then death and Hades were thrown into the lake of fire. The lake of fire is the second death* (Revelation 20: 10,14).

This fascinating passage describing the final judgment of the dead is packed with insights into why Hell is inescapable. Without diving into the weeds of prophecy and an End Times debate that this book is not written to address, we should notice that Hell is **not** the lake of fire. Hell is *thrown* into the lake of fire. That's a very meaningful and important distinction. The lake is made of burning sulfur and fire, and Hell – the place where souls are condemned – is hurled right in the middle of it.

Dr. Evans uses the brilliantly composed analogy of

the famous, though now shuttered, maximum-security prison in San Francisco Bay called Alcatraz.[4] From 1934 to 1963 its residents knew it as "The Rock." Designed to house the most notorious criminals, Alcatraz Island became home to murderers, rapists, and gangsters. Al Capone, "Machine Gun" Kelly, "The Birdman" of Alcatraz, and Roy Gardner all spent time imprisoned on the island.

Gardner even wrote a book about his experiences there that he called, "Hellcatraz: the Rock of Despair." He wrote that conditions were so horrific that it was literally a "tomb of the living dead."[5]

While it was open, 36 inmates attempted to escape from the prison – none survived. Only 7 of the 36 escaped the cell walls to the waters surrounding the island, and each of them either drowned or were eaten alive in the heavily shark-infested bay. Asked the worst part of The Rock, most inmates would point across the water to the bright lights of the free, vibrant city of San Francisco – so close they could hear the sounds of music and laughter, yet impossible to reach.

The similarities between that imprisoned island and what the Bible teaches about Hell are astonishing:

- Alcatraz was designed for the worst enemies of the state.
- Hell was designed for the worst enemies of God.

- Prisoners of Alcatraz dwell there with all the others who rebelled against the authority of man's law.
- Prisoners of Hell dwell there with all the others who rebelled against the authority of God's law.

- Not all prisoners on Alcatraz were equal; depending on their offenses, they were held in maximum, medium, or minimum security cells.
- Not all prisoners of Hell are equal; depending on their offenses, they receive maximum, medium, or minimum punishments.

- A large, shark-infested San Francisco Bay prevented any hope of escape from Alcatraz.
- A large, lava-filled lake of fire prevents any hope of escape from Hell.

The parallels are significant, but of course, there is one obvious, terrifying distinction. Reading the correspondence, letters, testimony, and statements of those who were confined on the prison island, there are consistent refrains of hope in the midst of their despair. Some write of how the sunlight through their cell windows went from being a taunting reminder of lost freedom to a cherished part of their day. Others speak of the conversations and camaraderie they were able to develop with fellow inmates, commiserating together over a terrible meal or across the stone hallways at night. And still more wrote about the rumored closing of Alcatraz and the hope for a transfer.

In Hell there will be none of that. There will be no sunshine, there will be no commiserating in conversation. All there will be is an eternal awareness that the darkness and isolation will endure forever without end.

TWENTY-ONE

SOCIAL TORMENT

When I was a freshman in high school I developed a crush on a girl one year older than I was named Wendy. We would talk at school and in some of our similar classes, but when summer came and without the ability to drive, I was afraid that what I saw to be a budding relationship would wither and die. So I was thrilled when she called one Sunday afternoon and asked if I'd like to go with her to her church youth group that night. Of course I agreed.

Having grown up in a more traditional church setting, I was a little taken aback by the Pentecostal and expressive worship and singing that happened that night. But it was still a spirit-filled service that I was able to participate in. And then came the video. Following a short teen drama that imagined a tragic car accident that killed two of the kids in the skit, they turned the lights down and rolled a video that I will never forget.

It was a depiction of one of those teens waking up in heaven, surrounded by light, white, and a Jesus figure that exuded friendliness and grace. Then the music shifted and the screen turned dark. I don't mind admitting that I about had an accident in my chair when the next thing I heard was a blood-curdling scream, followed by a series of whips snapping, chains clanking, and what sounded like volcanic eruptions. Then more screaming.

Looking back now, I'm confident the special effects in the video were lacking, but as a young high school kid trying to impress a girl, I couldn't even feign amusement at what was unfolding. I was freaked out beyond belief watching this teenage soul ravaged with flames, running around the screen screaming unintelligible words, pleading for help. It was meant for shock value, no doubt, and the youth minister's purpose was to get our attention about the serious reality of Hell. And it got mine. I don't think I stopped thinking about that girl on the video for weeks.

But now in hindsight when I compare that video recreation to what I read in Scripture about souls in Hell, I can't say it was an overly accurate representation of what eternity would have been like for that lost teen. Take the words of Jesus when teaching about one such condemned soul:

The rich man also died and was buried. In Hades, where he was in torment, he looked up and saw Abraham far away, with Lazarus by his side. So he called to him, 'Father Abraham, have pity on me and send Lazarus to dip the tip of his finger in water and cool my tongue, because I am in agony in this fire' (Luke 16:22-24).

A couple things I notice about this rich man:

1. He was not on fire himself or, as that poor girl in the video was experiencing, having flames burst outward from within his fire-consumed soul.
2. He speaks coherently and rationally rather than babbling nonsense in some semi-conscious state of mind.

What that tells me is that Hell is not a torture chamber. Instead, as other translations of these verses from Luke say, it is a state of torment. Combine this and a couple other passages, and a pretty coherent picture emerges of the various forms that this torment takes.

First, the social torment. Look back at the verses from Luke to see what I think is their most terrifying aspect. It's not the agony, the fire, the heat, or the thirst. It's these six words: *He looked up and saw Abraham* (Luke 16:23).

Think about the Alcatraz parallel and remember that the inmates there almost all testified how torturous it was to see the energy, nightlife, and even hear the music of San Francisco float across the bay to their eyes and ears. They could look out at where they could have been had they simply made different choices.

It is clear from this passage that the window between Heaven and Hell seems to be a one-way mirror of sorts. Perhaps the most tormenting part of Hell is being able to look at where you could have been but will never be. That daily, moment-by-moment reminder of what Heaven is, and that you'll never be able to go, is a social torment of separation that is hard to fathom.

That's why even when you consider that some who go to Hell will not be as bad of sinners and therefore will not face the same kinds of punishment, it remains an unthinkable end: you're still on the same "Rock," and you're still seeing the same shoreline that you can never reach. Being eternally reminded of what you missed simply because you inexplicably rejected God's free offer to save you is too terrible to even contemplate.

And there's one more aspect to this that makes it even worse. Remember I mentioned this was a one-way mirror. Here's how we know:

See, I will create new Heavens and a new

WHEN THE BEGINNING ENDS
WHAT HAPPENS WHEN WE DIE?

Earth, the former things will not be remembered, nor will they come to mind (Isaiah 65:17).

In the Heaven and New Earth that God is making for those who choose Him, old painful memories of this life are wiped clean and made new. But in Hell there is no such relief. In Hell we will experience eternal regret at what might have, and should have been. We will watch those we knew and loved enjoy the blessings reserved for saints while having their memories and recollections of us wiped from their minds.

Remember what Abraham said in response to the rich man's tormented request to have poor man Lazarus come cool his tongue:

But Abraham replied, 'Son, remember that in your lifetime you received your good things, while Lazarus received bad things (Luke 16:25).

Abraham would not be telling the rich man to "remember" his life if his tortured mind had been made new. Some folks desperately try to twist this truth into some sort of conciliation about Hell. If our memories remain, they reason, at least we'll know people and have the chance to reminisce. They paint a picture of Hell as a tavern full of sinners, drowning their sorrows for all eternity. This idea of a bad boy party in Hell was immortalized by the legendary rock group AC/DC when they belted out these well-known words:

> Don't need reason, don't need rhyme.
> Ain't nothing that I'd rather do.
> Goin' down, party time.
> My friends are gonna be there too.
> I'm on the Highway to Hell.[1]

I love the band and the raw vocals as much as the next guy, but I'm also smart enough to know that taking my understanding of the afterlife from a 1970s hard rock band preoccupied with being cool and rhyming words is not a great life decision. The Prophet Isaiah is a safer bet, and his characterization differs a tad from the rockers:

> *And they shall go forth, and look upon the carcasses of the men that have transgressed against Me; for their worm shall not die. Neither shall their fire be quenched; and they shall be an abhorring unto all flesh* (Isaiah 66:24).

As I've stated repeatedly, and probably to the point of annoyance, you can convince yourself whatever you want to believe about Hell. But Jesus has been there and the Scripture He affirmed tells us there is absolutely no social life in that terrible place. Will you have company? Absolutely. Will there be fraternity? Hardly.

Look back at Isaiah and notice that he says your

very existence will be an "abhorrence" to everyone else. Everyone around you will hate and despise you. Sorry AC/DC, the book of Daniel seconds this testimony from Isaiah:

> *Multitudes who sleep in the dust of the Earth will awake: some to everlasting life, others to shame and everlasting contempt* (Daniel 12:2).

Instead of abhorrence, Daniel chooses the word contempt. In Hell, people will be contemptuous to one another. That means there will be no allies, no teams, no factions, and no partners. You are on your own and everyone you encounter loathes you.

Think of people on Earth that you have accurately described to others in your life as having "no redeeming qualities." They seem to have no grace, no compassion, no understanding, not even moments of goodwill. Bingo – that is who is in Hell. That is the only kind of person who is in Hell, yourself included.

Why? Does God really make us extra-special evil to go there? No, God is not involved in this equation, and that is precisely the issue. In Hell people will express who they truly are apart from God's influence. If all our positive qualities of love, mercy, compassion, kindness – if all the good in our lives – is the result of God's presence, when that presence is removed we will exhibit none of those qualities. Everybody will repulse everybody in Hell.

SOCIAL TORMENT – 21

You want to talk about torment for a social creature like man who feeds off of relationships and interaction, realize that no matter how many people are there, you will always be in solitary confinement. You will never have experienced loneliness like Hell.

TWENTY-TWO

PHYSICAL TORMENT

Whenever someone characterizes Hell, whether through a pop culture caricature or a scholarly, literary description, the one common theme that is never lacking is the representation of physical torture. From tiny devils with pitchforks jabbing the sides of fleeing souls, to the condemned falling off cliffs into a lava pool, to this horrifying description from Bill Wiese, the author who claims God sent him to Hell for 23 minutes so that he could tell everyone what it was like:

> Then the beast threw me against the wall. I crumbled onto the floor. It felt as though every bone in my body had been broken.' I felt pain, but it was as if the pain was being somehow softened. I knew I did not experience the full brunt of the pain. I thought, "How was it

blocked?"

The second beast, with its razor-like claws and sharp protruding fins, then grabbed me from behind in a bear hug. As it pressed me into its chest, its sharp fins pierced my back. I felt like a rag doll in its clutches in comparison to his enormous size. He then reached around and plunged his claws into my chest and ripped them outward. My flesh hung from my body like ribbons as I fell again to the cell floor. These creatures had no respect for the human body—how remarkably it is made. I have always taken care of myself by eating right, exercising, and staying in shape, but none of that mattered as my body was being destroyed right before my eyes.

I knew that I could not escape this torture via death, for not even that was an option. Death penetrated me, but eluded me. The creatures seemed to derive pleasure in the pain and terror they inflicted upon me.[1]

I find nothing in God's Word that suggests He is going to allow human beings like Bill to cross over the eternal divide, enter Hell, and then cross back into human life. I think the Bible paints as vivid a picture of eternal condemnation as one could ever need to be thoroughly convinced they don't want to go there. But clearly Mr. Wiese had some kind of experience that he believes is what Hell must be like. Frankly, if his account and warnings get other souls to think seriously about their eternal fate and move toward a saving relationship with Christ, I'm thrilled.

But here's what I will say about our human preoccupation with the physical torment of Hell: I think it's the least torturous aspect of the destination. I believe from Scripture that the social torment I described last chapter and the psychological torment I will detail in the next are far more dreadful and chilling than the physical anguish.

Yet there is certainly no denying that physical pain is a disturbing component of Hell. Remember in the earlier chapters about Heaven that we established that in the afterlife, our sensations of reality – what we experience with our senses – will be magnified immensely. We won't be semi-conscious spirit-souls floating around either the golden streets or the lava pits. We are in a heightened state of consciousness with our senses highly attuned to our surroundings – for good (Heaven) or ill (Hell). With that in mind, go back to the story of the afterlife that Jesus was recounting, and this time consider the physical implications:

> *In Hades, where he was in torment, he looked up and saw Abraham far away,*

with Lazarus by his side. So he called to him, "Father Abraham, have pity on me and send Lazarus to dip the tip of his finger in the water and cool my tongue, because I am in agony in this fire" (Luke 16:23-24).

In this small passage we discover that the rich man is seeing, hearing, talking, and feeling. Several chapters ago we found that in Heaven the saved are given eternal bodies made specifically for the experience. In Hell it will be no different – our bodies will be custom made for that place. Proof of that is offered both in Matthew 5 where Jesus refers to the "bodies" in Hell, and again in Revelation 20 where John discusses "bodies" being given up into the afterlife.

And what of the rich man's physical body? As I pointed out last chapter, he isn't writhing around incapable of rational thought. He is not being consumed by fire or being thrown into stone walls by horrific beasts. He is engaging in rational, intelligent conversation, functioning in a thoughtful manner while testifying that he is in utter agony. What kind?

Several years ago before our youngest was born, we had taken our little girls to Disney World in the middle of the summer. Ordinarily we try not to go to central Florida during the hottest part of the year, but extenuating circumstances pushed our vacation into July that year. It was a particularly hot day with temperatures nearing 100, with the added humidity of Orlando making it feel much warmer. I remember standing in line for the Winnie-the-Pooh ride, which had recently placed their entire queue area under construction.

To protect guests from the work they were doing, Disney had built what amounted to a large wooden tunnel with fairly high walls and no roof that served as the line outside the ride building itself. It was about 3 pm, in the heat of the day, the sun beating down on us, and we were trapped in this claustrophobia-inducing tunnel with packs of people behind us and in front of us. I was holding our oldest child and Jenny was holding the younger. And there was no air moving.

I started to freak out. I couldn't find shade for Jenny to stand in, began to worry that I was going to overheat and leave her stranded with two kids and a lifeless cadaver of a husband right near Main Street, U.S.A. She kept reassuring me that we weren't too far from the entrance of the building where we would be out of the sun. But what she didn't know, what none of us knew, was that the ride was experiencing technical difficulties and the line wouldn't be moving for another 15 minutes.

I can say without hesitation that I never remember being that uncomfortable in my life. I've been in worse pain following a couple surgeries, but never in that kind of oppressive discomfort. I couldn't breathe and would have given anything for just the lightest of breezes or for some dude dressed up like Piglet to come walking through the line with a squirt bottle and shoot me in the face.

That's the closest I hope I ever am to understanding the kind of agony that the rich man found himself in – begging for a gentle breeze, a bit of shade, a drop of water. And unlike the happy ending to my story where we made it to ride Pooh in the cool air conditioning, this rich man's relief would never come. And in fact, according to Revelation, his desperation would only increase throughout eternity:

> *The fifth angel sounded his trumpet, and I saw a star that had fallen from the sky to the Earth. The star was given the key to the shaft of the abyss. When he opened the abyss, smoke rose from it like the smoke from a gigantic furnace. The sun and sky were darkened by the smoke from the abyss...the beast, which you saw, once was, now is not, and yet will come up out of the abyss and go to its destruction* (Revelation 9:1-2; 17:8).

Obviously, as we should expect with the book of Revelation, there is much in this passage relating to End Times prophecy. But my purpose in quoting these verses is to highlight the intentional reference to "the abyss." That word, properly translated, means an immeasurable place with no end. In modern language we would call it a bottomless pit.

Often people will refer to the sensation of falling and falling without end as a way to describe Hell. This reference to the endless abyss in Revelation is where that idea originates. And while I don't find that interpretation to be particularly irresponsible or wrong, its context also suggests a simpler explanation: that Hell is a place where things only get worse. The longing gets deeper, the pain never weakens, the futility increasingly consumes, and the wrath of God intensifies.

On Earth we experience a form of God's wrath – we've seen His power demonstrated in unrelenting waves overrunning shorelines as tsunamis. We've seen His fury in the toppling winds of hurricanes and tornados, the latter even dubbed "the finger of God." We've seen His ferocity exposed in skies splitting open with lightning. In every circumstance we as humans stand pitifully impotent to resist or shield ourselves from such incomparable might.

But on Earth, thankfully each of those demonstrations and spectacles of God's wrath are always tempered and restrained by the other attributes of God we enjoy – His compassion, patience, and provision. Hell on the other hand, is a world where God expresses only His wrath. No relenting, no tempering, no yielding. Remember, Hell is His divinely just retribution for the crime committed by Satan. For some reason, humans foolishly decide to involve themselves in the crossfire.

How dumb is that? Consider that even the Global Flood of Noah was tempered by God's redeeming love for the obedient and righteous – and yet it still wiped out the entire planet, upended the calendar and seasons, and forever altered Earth's geography. With no restraint, Hell will be far worse.

Jude warns: *They are wild waves of the sea, foaming up their shame; wandering stars, for whom blackest darkness has been reserved forever* (Jude 13). How bad is this un-tempered wrath of God? You will never see a sunrise. Just as in Heaven there is no night because of the brilliance of God's goodness, in Hell there is no day because of its absence.

But there's still more. If we desire a true glimpse of what Hell is like, there is one more torment that is explicitly clear in Scripture that cannot be overlooked. And I believe it is the worst Hell has to offer.

Yes, loneliness and social isolation is terrible. It is on Earth and will be much more so in Hell. And yes, physical pain is awful both on Earth and in its heightened state in Hell. But being at war and never finding peace *in your own mind* – psychological torment – is simply a debilitating and an unbearable torture for countless souls here in this life.

Take that horror, remove the presence of God, which Hell does, and it gets frighteningly, immeasurably worse.

TWENTY-THREE

PSYCHOLOGICAL TORMENT

The summer between my first and second year teaching was one of the most difficult times in my life. What started as a physical reaction to an unexpected drop in my body's potassium level during a family vacation soon devolved into my first struggle with anxiety.

And as anyone who has dealt with an anxiety disorder can attest to, the last thing you are willing to accept is the idea that the problems you experience are mental or psychological in nature. I was convinced it had to be more than that, and spent an incredible amount of money to pay for a full battery of tests to figure out the source of my problem. After my arms had bruised up from all the blood draws and needle sticks for fluids, every test had come back fine. By every medical measure I was perfectly healthy, but I remained convinced the doctors and medical professionals had to be missing something.

My doctor kept assuring me that I was physically well – no heart problem, no tumors, no blood pressure issues, no nerve problems. He kept patiently encouraging me to consider that my complications were psychological or psychosomatic. "The mind is an incredibly powerful thing," he continued to repeat. I wouldn't accept it though and continued seeking out different tests to explain why I was getting that short-of-breath, fingers-crawling-up-the-back-of-my-neck sensation.

I would sit in my apartment and stare at the wall for hours just waiting for those feelings to return again. When they did, my heart rate would go crazy, my breathing would get rushed – it was miserable. After two months of that, I finally conceded that maybe my doctor was right. I let him prescribe some anxiety pills for me to take, and I took them.

But I also wanted counseling. If it was a mental problem, I wanted to defeat it mentally. The counselor I met with unsurprisingly affirmed exactly what my doctor had told me: the human mind is incredibly powerful and fascinatingly complex. To ease my sense of shame, he showed me statistics of the shocking number of Americans who are dealing with some form of anxiety and psychological torment. He also talked to me about the very real chemical imbalance that can happen in some people's brains that leads to more serious forms of anxiety, including depression.

I learned a lot about the inordinate power of the human mind that summer. And while I have never experienced anything on par with those eight weeks of basically sitting paralyzed on my couch waiting to have another nervous meltdown, I'd be lying if I didn't admit that I don't always manage my stress levels responsibly and it can lead to moments of panic and anxiety even to this day. I'm guessing it will be a thorn in my side my entire life.

I say all that because understanding the debilitating effect that psychological torment can have on a person is essential in grasping the most terrifying aspect of Hell, at least in my estimation. In the Gospel of Mark, Jesus warns,

> *It is better for thee to enter life maimed, than having two hands to go into Hell, into the fire that never shall be quenched: where their worm dieth not, and the fire is not quenched* (Mark 9:43-44).

I used the older King James translation of that verse because the language is actually far more accurate than what the New International Version offers – and in this case it makes a significant difference. In this passage, Jesus is quoting from the prophet Isaiah who was speaking of God's final judgment of unbelievers. Notice two things about "the worm" mentioned here:

1. It is singular – one worm (that is what the NIV misstates)
2. It is personal – it is "their" worm, not a general "the" worm

Whatever this "worm" is that is being referenced, it is an instrument of personal, internal torment as opposed to the external torment of fire discussed last chapter. So what is the "worm?" As gross as this may be to you, it's important to have an understanding of what happens to our physical bodies when they are laid in the grave. Eventually the worms of death come and find us – the maggots and microbes find a way to get into your casket, no matter how well sealed it is.

But after they've done their work eating our dead body, they themselves die. They feed off of death and then experience it themselves. But this worm of the 2nd death (Hell), according to God's Word, never dies. And since we know that worm is personal and internal, that means the internal torment of Hell is everlasting.

What is this internal torment? It's an eternity of remembering it didn't have to be this way; an eternity of recalling all the times God was knocking at the door to your life and you ignored Him; an eternity of reliving all the times you scoffed or laughed at your need for a Savior and the sacrificial work of Christ; an eternity of guilt that never leaves or lessens. We see that happening with the rich man in the story Jesus tells:

> But Abraham replied, 'Son, remember that in your lifetime you received your good things, while Lazarus received bad things, but now he is comforted here and you are in agony' (Luke 16:25).

While the sufferings of the old life are wiped clean for those new creations in Christ that walk the streets of Heaven, the painful memories remain for those in Hell. Notice that what Abraham is saying to the rich man isn't broad or generic platitudes about the missed opportunity to accept God's gift of grace. These are specific memories that were personal to him. And if his memories were personal, that means ours will be as well.

It also confirms the important but often overlooked truth that Hell is not the same for everyone. Or maybe it would be better if I said not everyone *experiences* the same things in Hell. Jesus taught this plainly:

> And you, Capernaum, will you be lifted to the Heavens? No, you will go down to Hades. For if the miracles that were performed in you had been performed in Sodom, it would have remained to this day...Truly I tell you, it will be more bearable for Sodom and Gomorrah on the Day of Judgment than for that town

(Matthew 10:15, 11:23).

The explanation of that is fairly self-evident; it will be worse for some in Hell than others. I think sometimes one of the reasons the book of Revelation seems so intimidating to people is because they try to understand the whole drama of the end times at once. If we would discipline ourselves to look at isolated passages, we would see how perfectly they fit with what Jesus Himself was teaching about the afterlife. For instance,

> *And I saw the dead, great and small, standing before the throne, and books were opened. Another book was opened, which is the book of life. The dead were judged according to what they had done as recorded in the books* (Revelation 20:12).

Coupled with everything Jesus has told us about eternity, this is not a difficult passage to understand. When someone rejects Jesus as the way to heaven, they are essentially saying to God, "Judge me on my works, I'm doing this on my own." If you aren't pleading the blood of Jesus to cover over your works, you are necessarily standing before the Judge on the basis of those works, asking for admittance into heaven.

Your refusal to accept Jesus judges where you go, but the book of life that records your deeds then determines your place or status in that location (Heaven or Hell). That's why Christ could say it will be more bearable for Sodom than for Capernaum. Because according to the record of their works, while both were evil, Capernaum had far more opportunity and reason to repent and be redeemed. Their sin was greater, thus their punishment will be greater.

That's also why those souls who protest our urgent warnings about Hell by reasoning with us that they are "good people" and therefore shouldn't have anything to fear, are tragically misinformed. What they mean is that they aren't murderers, rapists, thieves, or swindlers. They do some bad stuff like everybody, but they are generally decent human beings. Therefore, in their estimation, any just God couldn't send them to the same place that He sends serial killers.

The truth is that they are headed for a different fate than those serial killers, but not a different place. They may be receiving a minimum-security cell, but they will still be in the eternal Alcatraz, separated from God for eternity because that is what they have chosen.

While the degree of your punishment in Hell is predicated upon *how bad you were*, your residency in Hell is not; it's predicated on *if you were bad*. And since God is the standard of goodness we must attain in order to not be considered bad, we are all bad (Romans 3:23).

That means apart from salvation in Christ alone, we have chosen an eternity in Hell – even those of us who pridefully compare our deeds to people we know commit worse ones. When we do that we are tragically setting ourselves up for an eternity of psychological torment over those "small wrongs" that we let keep us from Heaven.

Truthfully, the most psychologically devastating reality of Hell is that it is a place where your sin nature is set free to rule over you, but like Jesus said, it will never be satisfied or quenched. On earth, those who sin sexually have a release. Those who are addicted to drugs have a fix. Those who are filled with rage have their victims.

In Hell, just like the rich man who craved water with no satisfaction, the sexually immoral will feel that unrestrained predatory urge but without any way to satisfy it. The addict will still crave his fix, but will be unable to find it. The man overrun by anger will be unable to control his temper, yet everyone he encounters in Hell will make him angrier than the last. There will be no distractions from our sinful desires – they will consume us. There will be no substitutes for their fulfillment, meaning the gnawing of that worm will never end.

In James we are reminded that *every good and perfect gift is from above* (James 1:17). In Hell, the goodness of God is absent. There is no anticipation of anything because there are no gifts. There are no dreams and ambitions because there is no accomplishment. There are no goals or aspirations because there will be no achievements. It is a land of despairing futility.

And given that it is eternal separation from the Prince of Peace, *there is no peace for the wicked* (Isaiah 48:22). It is precisely what that preacher told me when I asked him to give me a picture of Hell. It is the return of the Genesis 1:2 earth – a void and barren landscape, forsaken and empty, where those who dwell have no purpose, no meaning, and no hope.

If that alone doesn't terrify you, I would dare suggest that you may be in grave danger of having to experience it for yourself.

TWENTY-FOUR

HOW COULD HE?

So this is it. This is the last chapter I will write in this book. Not because there isn't a lot more I think, a lot more I tend to believe, a lot more I'd like to throw out as real possibilities when it comes to Heaven, Hell, and what happens to us after this beginning phase of our immortality ends and the real living begins.

But I have set out in this book to speak only where the Bible speaks, say and conclude only what the Bible allows. And in that sense I'm almost satisfied. Almost. There's a reason why 76% of the American population claims to believe in Heaven, but only 6% of that same population claims to believe in Hell. We simply can't reconcile how a truly loving God could ever allow the existence of such a terrible place.

It's important to be reminded of a few truths whenever this nagging question emerges.

WHEN THE BEGINNING ENDS
WHAT HAPPENS WHEN WE DIE?

1. Hell was designed for Satan and his angels, not for people.
2. God is eternal, and making us in His image, He gave us an immortal, eternal soul.
3. He made mankind eternal so that we could live forever with Him.
4. We chose to rebel and separate ourselves from Him. Given our eternal nature, that would mean eternal separation.

If that was the pitiful state of humanity, let's test our own sense of morality and ask, what would a loving God do to fix things? Though He wants to, He can't live for eternity with us because of the irreconcilable conflict between His perfect nature and our decision to choose a sinful nature. So to remedy the hopeless situation we put ourselves in, out of no obligation besides His unfathomable love for His human family, God offered a way out. A substitute. He offered One who didn't owe any debt of sin for Himself – the only acceptable alternative. I can't take on your debt if I'm in debt myself. Jesus wasn't in debt.

Jesus would bear the sins that separated us from God, and bury them in Hell. What would a loving God do? Exactly that. He would offer a way out that costs us nothing but the choice to accept. Understanding that truth, now pause to consider our arrogance for just a second:

- We screwed up God's design.
- We intentionally chose to rebel against Him.

- We chose an eternity with Satan over an eternity with Him.
- God offers to fix things for us, and sacrifices His own perfect Son on our behalf.
- He says to us, "Even in your sinful rebellion that hurt Me, I am offering you the nail scarred hand of my Son. Take it, and let me lift you into paradise."
- We respond by pushing Christ's hand away, pouting, and questioning how God could even think about letting us go to Hell if He really loved us.

Astounding haughtiness! Egotistical conceit that knows no limits! Pride that should drag us to the pit of eternal Hell! And yet there remains one force that can still outreach it all – the love of the Father.

Many times I will hear atheists taunts or read unbelievers write mocking statements like, "You Christians have been watching the sky for Jesus to return for 2,000 years! Did He forget the way? What's He waiting for?"

Here's a thought. Maybe He's waiting for them. Maybe His delay is nothing less than yet another further demonstration of the long-suffering patience of a God desperate to provide us every chance to choose eternity with Him over eternity in Hell.

The author of Hebrews begs us, *Today, if you hear His voice, do not harden your hearts as you did in rebellion* (Hebrews 3:15). Why? Because today could

WHEN THE BEGINNING ENDS
WHAT HAPPENS WHEN WE DIE?

be the last day the offer is made to you, to me, to all of us.

Several years ago I picked up the book *Crazy Love* by Francis Chan. In it he recounts one of the most remarkable stories I have ever heard about a funeral service he performed for a man named Stan Gerlach:

> As a pastor, I'm often called upon when life "vanishes like a mist." One of the most powerful examples I've seen of this was Stan Gerlach, a successful businessman who was well known in the community. Stan was giving a eulogy at a memorial service when he decided to share the gospel. At the end of his message, Stan told the mourners, "You never know when God is going to take your life. At that moment, there's nothing you can do about it. Are you ready?" Then Stan sat down, fell over, and died. His wife and sons tried to resuscitate him, but there was nothing they could do--just as Stan had said a few minutes earlier.
>
> I'll never forget receiving that phone call and heading over to the Gerlach house. Stan's wife, Suzy, was just arriving home. She hugged me and cried. One of her sons, John, stepped out of the car weeping. He asked me, "Did you hear

the story? Did you hear? I'm so proud of him. My dad died doing what he loved doing most. He was telling people about Jesus."

I was asked to share a word with everyone gathered. There were children, grandchildren, neighbors, and friends. I opened my Bible to Matthew 10:32-33: "Whoever acknowledges me Before men, I will also acknowledge him before my Father in heaven. But whoever disowns me before men, I will disown him before my Father in heaven."

I asked everyone to imagine what it must have felt like for Stan. One moment, he was at a memorial service saying to a crowd, "This is who Jesus is!" The next, he was before God hearing Jesus say, "This is who Stan Gerlach is!" One second he was confessing Jesus; a second later, Jesus was confessing him![1]

I would regret not asking you if you had your Stan Gerlach moment as you finish these pages, would Jesus be confessing your name? *Or do you show contempt for the riches of His kindness, forbearance and patience, not realizing that God's kindness is intended to lead you to repentance* (Romans 2:4)?

WHEN THE BEGINNING ENDS
WHAT HAPPENS WHEN WE DIE?

I'm in full agreement with many of the men I have researched and read for this book that the two words that will be heard all over Hell for eternity are, "If only."

It doesn't have to be that way. For anyone. One of the most difficult concepts to grasp about Christianity is really one of the easiest in theory. It's called grace.

When my wife and I started dating seriously, we had many conversations about our spiritual growth. Jenny had convinced herself through unnecessary guilt over youthful indiscretions that she had been drifting in her faith while I had been becoming some bulwark of spirituality. I didn't realize how serious her misperceptions were until she verbalized her fear that she might not make it into heaven.

I pressed her on that. "Haven't you surrendered your life to Jesus? Weren't you obedient to His plan of salvation as laid out in Scripture?" She laughed and said that of course she had done that, but was just worried because I was so much "better of a person" than her. I hadn't done some of the things she had done. I knew a lot more about Christianity and the Bible than her. Certainly on the topic of God's grace, she was proving that last point to be true. She didn't get it. (For the record, she's getting better about that. But as many Christians know, accepting that God loves you so much to offer undeserved grace is harder than you might think).

Here's the truth that I expressed to her on numerous occasions and continue to express to anyone who will listen: I'm not going to heaven because I'm a good man. I'm not a good man. Even with my best efforts I'm not a good man. I'm a sinner. Sometimes many times over. There's no way my character gets me into heaven.

Instead, I've banked everything – my eternal soul – on the substitutionary death, burial, and resurrection of Jesus.

When the book of life is opened one day, spilling out all of my secrets and displaying all the filthy rags that others and I so often mistake on this earth as righteousness, you will see me waving my white flag of surrender. "No, Father, I come with no merit, no right to be here. I come only on the invitation of your Son. I'm with Him."

And Jesus will rise, approach the scales of eternal justice weighing so heavily against me, and tip them to my favor with just one drop of His blood. He will take me by the hand and He will usher me through the gates of my new home.

That is how my beginning will end. What about yours?

I accepted Christ as my Savior on January 1st, 1985

CITATIONS

Unless specifically noted, all Scripture references in each chapter are taken from the New International Version and King James Version of the Holy Bible using the online resource BibleGateway.com, a service of:

Zondervan Corporation
3900 Sparks Drive SE
Grand Rapids, MI 49546

Chapter Two

[1] Hochman, David. "Reinvent Yourself: The Playboy Interview with Ray Kurzweil," *Playboy*, April 19, 2016. Online: https://www.playboy.com/articles/playboy-interview-ray-kurzweil.
[2] Brodwin, Erin. "The 700-calorie breakfast you should eat if you want to live forever, according to a futurist who spends $1 million a year on pills and eating right," *Business Insider*, April 13, 2015. Online: http://www.businessinsider.com/ray-kurzweils-immortality-diet-2015-4.

Chapter Three

[1] Larry King Now, episode available online: https://www.youtube.com/watch?v=Ndj5KjKyr3E&t=358s.
[2] Oprah Winfrey Network, episode available online: https://www.youtube.com/watch?v=keSCaQQzoLc.
[3] The Atheist Voice, episode available online: https://www.youtube.com/watch?v=-6tLsO5bchU.
[4] Oprah Winfrey Network, episode available online: https://www.youtube.com/watch?v=Se26xa1AtUs&t=114s.

[5] Big Think, episode available online:
https://www.youtube.com/watch?v=ziwDvejyrA0.
[6] Oprah Winfrey Network, episode available online:
https://www.youtube.com/watch?v=5TbIEaWL0Eg.

Chapter Five

[1] Video available at CrystalKernan.com.
[2] Evans, Tony. *The Afterlife, Glimpses of Heaven and Hell* (The Urban Alternative: Dallas, TX), 2013.

Chapter Seven

[1] Hitchens, Christopher. *The Portable Atheist: Essential Readings for the Nonbeliever* (Da Capo Press: Philadelphia), 2007.
[2] Evans, Tony. *The Afterlife, Glimpses of Heaven and Hell* (The Urban Alternative: Dallas, TX), 2013.

Chapter Eight

[1] "The Alternate Side." *Seinfeld*. NBC. December 4, 1991, TV.

Chapter Nine

[1] Mann, Adam. "How to Picture the Size of the Universe," *Wired Magazine*, December 6, 2011. Online: https://www.wired.com/2011/12/universe-size/.

Chapter Eleven

[1] Evans, Tony. *The Afterlife, Glimpses of Heaven and Hell* (The Urban Alternative: Dallas, TX), 2013.

Chapter Twelve

[1] Alcorn, Randy. "9 Facts About Heaven That Will Surprise You," *Lifeway*, February 29, 2016. Online: http://www.lifeway.com/Article/pastor-Questioning-heaven.

Chapter Fifteen

[1] Evans, Tony. *The Afterlife, Glimpses of Heaven and Hell* (The Urban Alternative: Dallas, TX), 2013.

Chapter Sixteen

[1] Chan, Francis. "Erasing Hell by Francis Chan," video available online: https://www.youtube.com/watch?v=qnrJVTSYLr8&t=310s.
[2] Serial Killer Crime Index, "Bill Benefiel," content available online: http://www.crimezzz.net/serialkillers/B/BENEFIEL_bill_j.php.

Chapter Seventeen

[1] Evans, Tony. *The Afterlife, Glimpses of Heaven and Hell* (The Urban Alternative: Dallas, TX), 2013.

Chapter Eighteen

[1] Chan, Francis. *Erasing Hell* (David C. Cook: Colorado Springs, CO), 2011.

Chapter Nineteen

[1] Edwards, Jonathan. "The Miscellanies": (Entry Nos. a-z, aa-zz, 1-500) *WJE Online* Vol 13, Ed. Harry S. Stout, 1722. Online: http://edwards.yale.edu/archive?path=aHR0cDovL2Vkd2FyZHMueWFsZS5lZHUv Y2dpLWJpbi9uZXdwaGlssby9nZXRvYmplY3QucGw/Yy4xMjo0OjE6MTQyLndqZW8=.
[2] Evans, Tony. *The Afterlife, Glimpses of Heaven and Hell* (The Urban Alternative: Dallas, TX), 2013.
[3] The New Yorker. "A Megachurch Pastor's Search for a More Forgiving Faith," *The New Yorker Magazine*, December 16, 2016. Online: http://www.newyorker.com/culture/culture-desk/a-megachurch-pastors-search-for-a-more-forgiving-faith.

Chapter Twenty

[1] Saint Teresa, and Benedict Zimmerman. *The Life of St. Teresa of Jesus of the Order of Our Lady of Carmel* (Benziger Brothers: New York), 1916.
[2] Plese, Matthew. *Eschatology: The Catholic Study of the Last Four Things* (The Goldhead Group: Raleigh, NC), 2015, quoting Sister Lucy of Fatima.
[3] Wiese, Bill. *23 Minutes In Hell* (Charisma House: Lake Mary, FL), 2006.
[4] Evans, Tony. *The Afterlife, Glimpses of Heaven and Hell* (The Urban Alternative: Dallas, TX), 2013.
[5] Gardner, Roy. *Hellcatraz: The Rock of Despair*, 1938.

Chapter Twenty-One

[1] AC/DC. *Highway to Hell*. Highway to Hell. By Angus Young, Malcolm Young, and Bon Scott. Produced by Mutt Lange, 1979. Vinyl.

Chapter Twenty-Two

[1] Wiese, Bill. *23 Minutes In Hell* (Charisma House: Lake Mary, FL), 2006.

Chapter Twenty-Four

[1] Chan, Francis. *Crazy Love* (David C. Cook: Colorado Springs, CO), 2008.

Made in the USA
Lexington, KY
08 May 2019